"With the ever-increasing number of extensive treatments of the Enneagram we are in need of a book like this; it has all the essentials expressed with admirable brevity. This book is a clear, insightful, and very concrete presentation of the Enneagram. Its unique value lies in the way it shows how the insight that the Enneagram gives into our human weakness and waywardness can become a very constructive experience. As a result of reading it, I am a lot clearer about the meaning of Carl Jung's statement that the shadow is 90 percent gold."

Peter Hannan, S.J.
Author, *Nine Faces of God*

"The authors explain the Enneagram well, then position it properly as a tool. Where they really shine is in their use of Scripture. It's hard to integrate the biblical stories and the Enneagram energies, but they do a far better than average job of it. This will be a help to spiritual directors who take their Scriptures seriously."

Clarence Thomson
The Enneagram Educator

"Fitzgerald and Bergin have written a book about the Enneagram that is short, simple, and real. Their concise and clear presentation will aid both the novice and the veteran in understanding the Enneagram. Particularly helpful are the identity cards with their simple outlines and clear explanations. Their emphasis on the spirituality aspect adds a needed dimension to the psychological explanation."

Loretta Girzaitis
Enneagram Director
Victorious Spirit Enterprises

"This basic guide to understanding the Enneagram combines brevity and simplicity with a well-grounded sense of the real life concerns of believers. Of the many introductory books on the Enneagram available, none is easier to understand or more cognizant of the spiritual dimension. Among the many interesting features of the book is an Enneagram test which is composed of 25 statements for each type. You simply check the statements in each type that apply to you and tally the score under each type to get an initial sense of where you belong.

"Readers who are interested in learning about the Enneagram for the first time and those who would like to introduce others to it will find this a most valuable resource."

Spiritual Book News

"A clear presentation of the basics of the Enneagram, the self-discovery method. The authors propose a special prayer for each of the personality types, along with selected scriptural passages to bring inspiration and solace to all."

Pat Durbin
The Catholic Times

"I found the approach to healing and spirituality in *An Enneagram Guide: A Spirituality of Love in Brokenness* both clear and profound. It will be a useful tool and introduction for many people."

John Heagle, M.A., J.C.L.
Co-Director, TARA Center

AN ENNEAGRAM GUIDE

A *Spirituality of Love in Brokenness*

Éilís Bergin PBVM
Eddie Fitzgerald SDB

TWENTY-THIRD PUBLICATIONS
Mystic, Connecticut 06355

SDB MEDIA
Dublin, Ireland

Fifth printing 2000

Cover illustration by H. Grabowski

Published in Ireland by SDB Media
St. Teresa's Rd.
Dublin 12
Phone: (01) 555605
Fax: (01) 558781
ISBN 0-948320-09-5

and in North America by

Twenty-Third Publications/Bayard
185 Willow Street
P.O. Box 180
Mystic CT 06355
(860) 536-2611
(800) 321-0411

ISBN 0-89622-564-X
Library of Congress Catalog Card Number 93-60209

CONTENTS

AN ENNEAGRAM GUIDE

INTRODUCTION

The Inner Journey

A few years ago we were told a story by a lecturer in communications which in many ways illustrates some of the things we will be dealing with in this book. He was talking with a group of students one day about interviewing techniques and invited a few of them to do some mock interviews. Understandably, not one interview came alive.

"Look," said John, "everyone has a story inside them. It's up to you to get it out. For example, I could go out into the street, take the first person I met, bring him or her in here, and in five minutes get something that would knock your socks off."

"All right," replied one of the students, "we dare you!"

John looked at them quietly for a moment and then took up the challenge. When he opened the door he found a delivery boy with a grin on his face. He asked him if he'd be good enough to come inside and allow himself to be interviewed for a few minutes. The young fellow agreed and was soon sitting quite happily in front of a fascinated group of students.

For a few minutes John asked him some questions about his job, about the traffic, and about the people he met. Then John stopped for a moment and said gently, "Dave, we've been talking here for the past five minutes and you haven't stopped smiling once. Could you tell me why?"

"Well, if you really want to know," replied Dave, "I'll tell you. When I was born I had something like a harelip. My mouth wasn't quite right and my mother was very upset. Eventually she got me to the hospital and I had an operation to put it right, but the operation went wrong. So now I have a smile on my face all day long. Many people think that's marvelous. But what I want to know is this: how do you tell people you're crying inside when you've got a permanent smile on your face?"

John said you could have heard a pin drop in the room. The tortured soul of a beautiful and sensitive human being was being revealed for a moment. A courier had come in off the street and taught a group of university students a lesson in life they would never forget.

Many of us are crying inside and others don't know anything about it. Indeed, some of us are crying inside and even we ourselves don't know about it. All too often we pass judgment on other people without ever really knowing what's happening within. Unfortunately, we frequently do the same to ourselves.

We're all scarred by life in some way. Those scars may be physical, emotional, psychological or spiritual, or, most probably, a subtle combination of some or all of them. We may try to hide our scars by putting a brave face on things, but the fact remains that inside we still experience our brokenness. Like Dave, we need to be listened to with respect; we need the love of people who don't judge by appearances but who take the time to get beneath the mask. We need empathy, not apathy. And we need this not only from others but primarily from ourselves.

It has been said that what we don't know can't hurt us. The problem is it can. The real truth is that what we don't know *does* hurt us! One of the principal reasons why we have problems in our personal lives is that we don't know who we are and what really motivates us. Many of us live on a superficial level and are content with that. But an essential part of our task in life is trying to understand what makes us tick. In doing so we begin to learn how to manage our lives better and how to improve our relationships with others.

About This Book

Without doubt, the best way to experience the transforming power of the Enneagram (pronounced *Enny*-a-gram) is on a person-to-person basis. This is generally done through individual counselling or by means of a workshop or course. Reading something on our own is one thing. Experiencing it in a group of differing personality types is quite another. Something happens to us in a group context which does not occur when we're studying on our own. The dynamic is different and so is what is learned. We learn from each other and actually see the types in action. When we're in a safe environment with experienced facilitators an extra dimension is added and we can experience the truth of the Enneagram with an immediacy and shared recognition which reading simply cannot give.

However, relatively few people have the opportunity of attending a workshop and fewer still are fortunate enough to have a counsellor to guide them. This is why books are important. They help reach a wider audience. They may be second best, but that is better than not sharing the richness of the Enneagram at all. In our own work with the Enneagram we don't believe in the cult of secrecy or the notion that writing about this helpful way of looking at people inevitably detracts from its significance. To do so would be both arrogant and divisive. The attempt to communicate and to share is fundamentally an attempt to unify and make whole. That is what prompts us to write.

Before we started to write this book, we asked many people what they thought was needed. In essence they suggested three things. It needs to be *short*—people don't want verbiage, they want to be able to focus their attention, not to have it diffused. It needs to be *simple*—they don't want complicated jargon or psychological mumbo-jumbo. And, most of all, it needs to be *real*—to be honest, sincere and grounded in lived experience. This is what we have tried to do here. We have tried to keep things brief without being skimpy, simple without being simplistic, and anchored to the real lives and genuine concerns of people today.

This book is meant for all those who want to experience the joy and freedom of living a life of inner peace and harmony, a life which is true to their best selves. What it has to offer is a way of understanding ourselves and others at depth, a way of appreciating the hidden compulsions which motivate us all, and a way of loving God in and through our love for ourselves and others.

1

TRAVELING LIGHT

The Enneagram is a complex and sophisticated tool for understanding personality types. In its essentials it is apparently a very ancient source of wisdom. From what little we know of its history it appears to have been transmitted by word of mouth, usually by a spiritual counselor to a disciple or person seeking enlightenment. It was used mainly as an agent of change, a way of conversion, so that people could begin to see themselves whole, learn to let go of their central compulsions and let God take control of their lives.

The exact origins of the Enneagram are probably now impossible to discover, but it would seem that for centuries it was preserved in this strictly oral tradition. The Sufi mystics, in particular, are said to have been instrumental in keeping the tradition alive. What we do know is that it eventually made its way from Afghanistan to the West by at least two separate routes. George Ivanovich Gurdjieff and Oscar Ichazo are both credited with its introduction, Gurdjieff in Europe and Ichazo first in Bolivia and Chile and then in the United States.

There's no doubt that we owe a great deal to the insights of Ichazo, whose pioneering work on the Enneagram has greatly influenced its modern development and presentation. His work was taken up by Claudio Naranjo in California and later by Rev. Robert Ochs and his fellow Jesuits, who quickly saw the help it could be in spiritual direction.

In the past thirty years or so it has been developed still further by others who have enhanced the tradition with many of the insights of modern psychology, particularly those of Carl

Jung. Now an increasing number of psychologists, psycho-analysts, management consultants, counsellors and spiritual directors are making use of it as both a therapeutic and pastoral tool in the course of their work.

Today it is no longer solely an oral tradition. There are many excellent books available on the subject. We ourselves are very grateful to all those who have shared their understanding of the Enneagram with us, whether as counsellors, lecturers, authors or fellow travelers on the inner journey. Many of these are mentioned in the bibliography at the back of this book. In particular we are indebted to all those who have attended our workshops and courses and who have helped us clarify our understanding of the different types by sharing their own stories and experiences with us.

A Heavy Load
The Enneagram is a method of self-discovery which helps people see themselves as they really are so that they can then allow their best selves to break through into the light. The word itself is relatively recent. It comes from the Greek *ennea* (nine) and *gramma* (point, letter or small weight) referring to the nine different personality patterns or types into which human beings can be divided.

On our journey through life we have managed to encumber and weigh ourselves down in one of nine different ways. From small beginnings we have succeeded in constructing a complex persona to hide behind. This mask becomes a real burden to us and effectively hinders our progress to psychological and spiritual maturity. The Enneagram helps us identify the masks we have fashioned and the reasons why.

But it does far more than give us a deeper understanding of our personality type. It also helps us to tap into the well-springs of strength, wisdom and love within each one of us. In doing so, it enables us to discover our truest selves, face up to our illusions, transcend our compulsions and liberate our special gifts. It is, therefore, an invaluable aid to personal development. It opens us to the possibility of change, so that we can begin to grow toward personal integration, real conversion and genuine spiritual wholeness.

It has been said that religion is for people who want to avoid hell, but spirituality is for those who have been there. We hope that our little contribution to the Enneagram will further its understanding as a way in which we can develop a spirituality of love in brokenness. We'll have more to say about this later on in the book, but it's worth noting here that in our team ministry we have found that holding out the possibility of discovering love in brokenness is a great help to people who find themselves living in their own private hell.

The Enneagram is about traveling light. It's a way of lifting the burdens from our shoulders and encouraging us to journey through life unencumbered. It helps us name our demons and encourages us to allow space for God to be God again in our lives. Little wonder, then, that those who have worked with it have found it to be such an invaluable guide on their spiritual journey.

Generally speaking, in the earlier part of life we put all our efforts into developing what we call our personality. We mark out our territory, fence off our ego-boundaries, and build our personal house. This then becomes the place where we feel most at home. The skills we have developed in constructing our personality enable us to feel more or less secure in a world which has become increasingly difficult and stressful to live in. So we get by, usually with a little help from our friends.

To the outside observer it might appear that all is well with us: we may have a comfortable house, a good job, an attentive spouse, healthy and contented children. "You've got it made," they say, and they're right. That's precisely what we've done. We've *made* our lives what they are today. We've adapted to both the crude and subtle influences of those with whom we've come in contact—particularly our parents, relatives, friends and colleagues. We've absorbed countless messages from our society, culture, religion and environment and succeeded in developing strategies which allow us to cope, more or less adequately, with the multiplicity of demands being made on us.

We may put a brave face on it, and for a while it may seem to work. But gradually we begin to experience a fundamental insecurity and know that we are both more than what we have made of ourselves, and also a great deal less.

Letting in the Light

When we get to mid-life most of us begin to discover from the inside that all isn't well and we start asking some very serious questions. Who are we, really? What makes us tick? How did we get to be the way we are? Where are we going? Is that all there is? This is the time when we are prompted to take our first steps on an inner journey of self-discovery which can bring us hope, courage and direction for the rest of our lives.

One of the great truths in life is that a journey of a thousand miles begins with the first step. It's a pity that so few of us are prepared to take the risk. Perhaps it's because we're afraid of the pain. But pain is an integral part of the growth process and forces us to answer questions we might not otherwise address.

We all need to undertake this inner journey and not be afraid of the effort and patience involved. All growth takes time and frequently involves hard work. The Enneagram would be worthless if it did nothing more than confirm us in our blindness. People whose eyes are opened to their real selves have a painful choice to make—either to keep their eyes open and let the process of change and renewal begin, or to close them tight once more, too scared of letting go of a self-image which has worked up until now but which has begun to bring an increasing amount of pain with it as the years have gone on.

In fact, there's nothing to be afraid of. Part of the adventure of the Enneagram is that it helps show us ourselves as we really are, not as we pretend to be. Little lights are switched on in the deepest reaches of our being so that we can see the beauty and giftedness which has been hidden away for so long. No doubt, there will also be dark areas which resist the coming of the light and are only transformed with patience and care. But, as we hope to make abundantly clear later on, God's love is often most clearly visible in and through our brokenness. There's no need to run away from the shadows when we live in the light of God's unconditional love.

In our next chapter we'll concentrate on the idea of personality types and explain some of the terms needed in familiarizing ourselves with this powerful agent for personal renewal known as the Enneagram.

2

PERSONALITY TYPES

There are many different ways of looking at human beings and trying to see what makes them tick. We all share an interest in this. Experience teaches us very quickly that in many respects we are different from everyone else. But we also note that there are certain ways of viewing reality and certain patterns of behavior which we have in common with some but not with others.

Attempts to describe or analyze these patterns or types have been made for thousands of years. For example, the Greek doctor Hippocrates, traditionally the embodiment of the ideal physician, saw human beings as being temperamentally one of four types—sanguinary, melancholic, choleric or phlegmatic. Modern psychologists find this both crude and very limiting, but in the fifth century B.C. it was probably very helpful.

There is a sense in which all attempts at understanding the variety of personalities which we see around us are bound to be rough-and-ready reductions of the splendid individuality of each and every person. We are learning more and more all the time about the complexity and originality of the person, and it is thanks to people like Hippocrates that we have been able to build up our knowledge and discover ever more sophisticated methods of looking at human beings.

The Enneagram is one of these ways of looking at the human personality. It suggests that there are nine basic personality types, based on nine differing compulsive energies, nine habitual inner fixations. These are identified and described with what many consider to be a great deal of clarity and sophistication.

Because they are clearly recognized as compulsions or motivating forces which drive us, there is an inner dynamic within the Enneagram model to encourage each personality to try to overcome the negative elements within their compulsive and narrow world view. That is why it has proved to be such a helpful tool for people looking for healing and personal growth and has been taken up by many spiritual directors as another aid which they offer to their clients in their search for wholeness and spiritual development.

It is very important to remind ourselves that no personality type is any better or any worse than the others. We all have our strengths and weaknesses. We all have a special gift and have been created to show forth one aspect of the "Face of God." But we all, too, have our brokenness. Within us all a voice cries out to be heard, challenging us to get in touch with our true selves and remain always open to the healing and conversion which God offers us every moment of our existence.

Moreover, depending on a wide variety of circumstances (among them family, education, culture, environment, etc.), each one of us finds ourselves more or less mature or immature, healthy or sick, integrated or alienated. People who belong to the same personality type may seem quite different from each other because one may be high up on the scale of integration and another low down. They can even present differently today from what they appeared to be yesterday, because a few hours can sometimes make all the difference between whether we are stressed or at peace. This is one good reason why the attempt to label people is both facile and foolish.

Numbers

The most common method of naming the various types is simply to give them each a number from one to nine. The reason for this is that the numbers are a convenient international shorthand for people who know the Enneagram so that they can talk about a particular personality type without continually having to go into detail.

The types could just as easily be identified by words like

Helper, Peacemaker, etc., but there is as yet no agreed single word for every type. For example, the type known as the SIX is variously called *Loyalist, Devil's Advocate, Guardian, Facilitator, Defender, Supporter,* and so on. These are all useful terms but in certain circumstances they can have their drawbacks. *Loyalist,* for example, captures well the pattern of loyalty of the SIX, but in a country like Ireland the word has become so politicized that it cannot be used without some confusion. All the other names, including our own, have their own peculiar drawbacks. This needn't prevent us from using them, but it makes sense to use numbers as well.

This does not mean that the Enneagram reduces us to a number. Far from it. The numbers simply refer to the blinkered and narrowly focused way in which the different personalities look at the world.

We must continually reject all efforts to label us, whether these come from others or, more subtly, from ourselves. As will be seen in the identity profiles we give in later pages, we have included a statement of identity for each of the personality types. Some people who do the Enneagram mistakenly think that the whole point is to identify themselves with their number. "I am a SEVEN and she is a SIX," they may say. However, this is a psychological cul-de-sac which produces no growth. All it does is provide us with another good reason for remaining just as we are—sleep-walking our way through life, stuck in the same old patterned rut we call our type. It simply reaffirms and reinforces the false notion that we *are* that pattern rather than that we *have* that pattern.

Each and every human being is completely and utterly unique. There has never been and never will be another precisely like us. Each one of us is different. It would, therefore, be insulting to think that our special selves could simply be reduced to a type or, worse still, to a number. We are not ciphers, we are distinct human beings. We rightly reject out of hand any attempt to strait-jacket our spirit or pigeonhole our personality in a pre-conceived category. Indeed, the whole point of the opening story of this book was precisely to indicate the respect we owe to the originality and sacredness of the individual.

The claim is sometimes made that the Enneagram is just another way of trying to get a quick fix on people, crudely categorizing them into a specific type and not allowing them to break out of that particular character mold.

This is a risk common to all typologies. In unsophisticated hands they can be misused in an attempt to pigeonhole people. To the extent that people use them simplistically, they grossly distort them. Over-simplification is always dangerous, particularly when it is combined with a blinkered attitude towards change.

Just because we have been given an insight into someone's compulsive behavior or inner drives does not mean we have anything like a full understanding of their personality. To equate a person with a compulsion is to short-circuit the knowledge to be gained from personal disclosure and interpersonal discovery. Moreover, to deny the possibility of change is in essence a refusal to accept the possibility of redemption.

There is no denying that inexperienced people have used both the Enneagram and other psychological theories to make snap judgments on people. For example, it's possible to hear people use phrases like: "I can't stand ONES, they're so uptight. She's a typical NINE, she won't budge. Be careful what you say, he's an out-and-out FOUR." However, this is more a criticism of the system itself. Every responsible teacher of the Enneagram warns not only of the dangers of over-simplification and snap judgments but of the mistake of identifying the person with the number.

The symbolic representation of the Enneagram is a circle with nine numbered points along its circumference. The numbers 3, 6, and 9 form an equilateral triangle while the other numbers are joined together in a six-sided figure (hexagon) in a recurring sequence: 1, 4, 2, 8, 5, 7. Mathematically these are the recurring decimal fractions which occur when the number 1 is divided by 7. The numbers and the names we use are to be found in Figure 1.

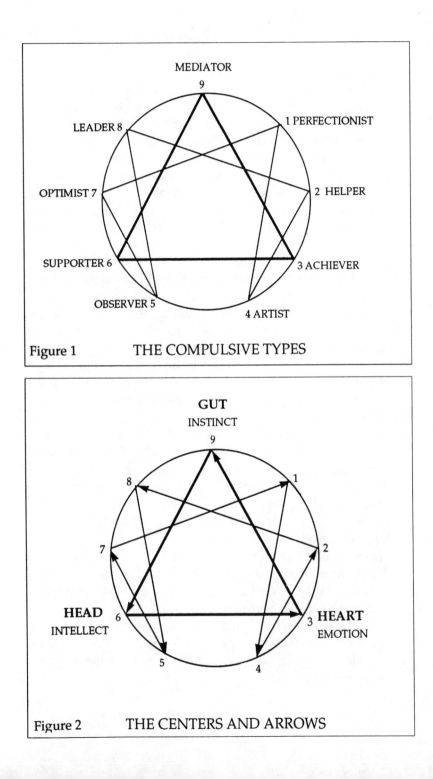

Figure 1   THE COMPULSIVE TYPES

Figure 2   THE CENTERS AND ARROWS

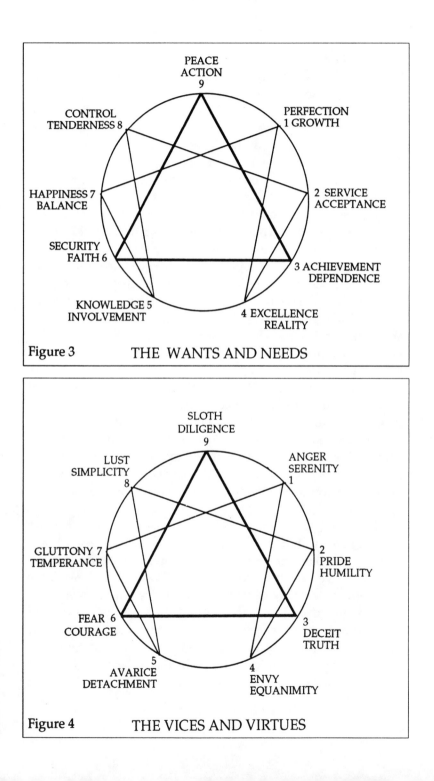

Figure 3   THE WANTS AND NEEDS

Figure 4   THE VICES AND VIRTUES

Compulsions

During our formative years we build up a set of fundamental assumptions about life and make them firmly our own. Eventually they're internalized so effectively that they become a fixed part of our subconscious. Because they're housed so deeply within us they can be extraordinarily powerful and effective motivating agents. Given their depth, they usually provide a more or less automatic trigger mechanism to the way we respond to people and events around us. In doing so they bring with them a certain feeling of security and a sense of being able to cope with various different life situations which become less threatening as a result.

How we relate with people and experience our environment from our earliest years determines the nature of our compulsive energy. This is one of the main reasons why children of the same parents can develop such completely different strategies for dealing with the world.

When we first approach the Enneagram we see part of ourselves in each of these types. This is because many types of people do more or less the same things. But the point is that they do them for quite different reasons. We can easily be mistaken in identifying our type when we concentrate on observable behavior or character traits rather than on the central compulsive energy which gives rise to them. It is when we go beyond these outward actions to our central fixation that we begin to see ourselves described most clearly as one particular type.

The central point here is not so much *what* we do but *why* we do it. It's really about our having created a self-image and then getting so locked into it that we don't want to break out of it and don't even see the need to do so. Early on in life we learn that certain things work for us and others don't. So we concentrate on what we see as advancing our survival, growth and development, become good at it and continue to overplay our hand since there seems no good reason not to do so at this stage.

There's a piece of folk wisdom which can sometimes be very helpful: "If it's not broken, don't fix it." Our problem with our compulsion is that it seems to work for us, so we think it doesn't need fixing. It's so much part of our lives that we can't see how broken it is, and how we have psychologically "fixed" ourselves within it. Effectively we're trapped in a construction of our own making. The sad part is that something *is* broken but we don't know it. We have been lulled into a false sense of security so that we turn a blind eye to what's really going on. And for many years we get away with it. We successfully avoid any attempts to call our bluff, to name our game.

What the Enneagram does is remind us that most of the time we act on automatic pilot, letting our built-in programming and compulsive navigational system take over the direction of how we behave, feel and think. It is only when we pull ourselves up short and reflect on what's going on inside that we begin to realize what's actually happening.

Inner Witness

There's a scene in the film *Ghost* where the hero is shot and his spirit is seen leaving his body and observing what happens when his wife and others attempt to revive him. We, too, need to learn to distance ourselves from our compulsions. We need to be able to step out of our egos and calmly observe what's going on both on the surface and within our psyche.

Most of us have had that experience from time to time. It's rather like watching a film of our own lives unfold on the screen before us, without the compulsiveness of our immediate involvement as one of the main characters. Right in the middle of an argument, for example, we may find an inner part of ourselves stepping back from the conflict, witnessing what's going on and commentating on the antics of the participants as if they were in a role-play situation.

That's what we mean by getting critical distance from ourselves. It's a letting go of our precious patterned responses which then frees us to see things from a different perspective. Humor also performs the same function. The ability to laugh at ourselves is very important and ought never to be underestimated.

This critical distance from ourselves helps liberate us from the bonds which tie us. This letting go of our ego allows us to see that certain things make us mad, sad, or glad. Above all, it allows us to ask the all-important question, "Why?" It gives us the breathing space to choose. If we have no choice we are not free. It's because we *are* free that we can change and develop. If we're trapped in a compulsion, addiction or fixation we're really in a kind of psychological prison.

The Enneagram encourages us to identify our personality type but not to identify *with* it. Change can only come about when we have first learned what we need to change *from*. To deal with our addictions we must first of all clarify what they are. Only then will we have a chance of doing something about them. Far from encouraging us to identify with our type, the Enneagram helps give us some distance from ourselves so that we can pay sympathetic attention to who we really are. We cannot allow ourselves to become too comfortable with our type. If we do so, we will never be truly free. The reality is that recognizing our type is only the beginning of a process of change, not the end.

Three Centers

Each one of us operates out of three different central energies—the *gut center*, the *heart center* and the *head center* (cf. Figure 2). When all three centers of energy are working in harmony our personalities are well-rounded and integrated. But most of us find that we tend to overuse one center, often at the expense of the other two. That center then becomes our preferred mode of operating.

We experience this every day of the week. We speak about some people as being "gutsy" or operating at "gut level"; the fire in their belly is what drives them on. We refer to others as being "all heart" or "bleeding hearts"; their feelings are what give them energy. And we see yet others as "eggheads" or as having their "head in the clouds"; their thoughts are the guiding force behind their deeds.

One way of finding out what our center of energy might be

is to imagine how we would react or respond in a crisis. Situations of stress or conflict frequently force us all to fall back on our preferred way of doing things, employing the central energy that comes quickest and easiest to us.

What would happen, for instance, if we saw a man beating a two-year-old child around the head in a shopping mall? In all probability we'd try to help the child. But, depending on our preferred center, we'd each do it differently. Let's allow ourselves to stereotype the three centers for a moment to make the point. This may well be a caricature of what would happen, but it is still largely recognizable as being characteristic of a particular kind of energy.

Those of us who operate primarily out of our *gut center* would probably not think twice (notice the phrase); we'd instinctively move to protect the child, if not give the man a dose of his own medicine. We'd probably act first and ask questions later. Our impulse to get involved would be so strong that we wouldn't even think about holding back. Our anger would probably blind us to the consequences of rushing in without weighing up the situation.

Those of us who operate primarily out of our *heart center* would no doubt be appalled by what was happening. Our heart would go out to the child, the weaker one, the one who should be nurtured and cared for. Our anxiety about the situation would increase very rapidly and we would feel there was nothing we could do but intervene. If our attempts to communicate with and placate the man failed, we'd let our heart rule our head and do what we had do in order to protect the child.

If, however, we operate primarily out of our *head center*, we'd have immediately taken in the situation and tried to make sense of it. Even though we might keep our distance and be somewhat fearful of getting involved, we'd certainly want to help the child. This would mean our analyzing all the possible options at our disposal, which we'd do with speed and clarity. If we noticed the police or a security guard or some other official in the vicinity we'd immediately enlist their help and encourage them to take charge. As a last resort we'd get involved ourselves, trying to reason with the man, get him to see sense—anything to calm him down so that we could rescue the child.

Centers and Types

In terms of the Enneagram each of these three central energies accounts for three quite different types of personality. If you think you are in the *gut center* you are likely to be an EIGHT (Leader), NINE (Mediator), or ONE (Perfectionist). If you find you are in the *heart center* you are probably a TWO (Helper), THREE (Achiever), or FOUR (Artist). And if you are in the *head center* you could be a FIVE (Observer), SIX (Supporter) or SEVEN (Optimist).

However, it's important to reflect on this for a while and not to be too quick to jump to the conclusion that you operate primarily out of one particular center.

In general the nine types are related to their center by whether they overemphasize, underplay or remain completely out of touch with it. Although there are subtleties and nuances to this, it would appear that the types relate to their center in the following ways.

The EIGHT, NINE and ONE types primarily tend to operate out of their *gut center*. This is essentially a hostile, "over-against" energy, an instinctual reaction, physical, sexual and confrontational in nature, concerned with power and justice. EIGHTS overemphasize their center, their natural style being to try to gain the upper hand, dominate and conquer. ONES underplay it, their natural style being to try to keep their aggressiveness under control while continuing to moralize and enforce their dogmatic ideas of right and wrong. NINES are very much out of touch with it, their natural style being to pour oil on troubled waters, to pacify, unite, and avoid vexation whenever possible.

The TWO, THREE and FOUR types primarily tend to operate out of their *heart center*. This is essentially a relational, "towards" energy, an emotional response, social and unifying in nature, concerned with image and relationships. TWOS over-emphasize their center, their natural style in relationships being to go out of their way to help others, especially those in need. However, in doing so they completely neglect their own feelings. FOURS underplay their center, their natural style in relationships being to withdraw into their inner life because they feel others just would not understand the incredible range of emotions they experience. Even though FOURS are highly involved in their own feelings, they tend to express them indirectly and artistically. THREES are very much out of touch with both their center and their feelings. Their natural style is to put all their energies into image-building. In the process they are willing to sacrifice their feelings and adapt their behavior to whatever will enhance this image.

The FIVE, SIX and SEVEN types primarily tend to operate out of their *head center*. This is essentially a withdrawing, "away from" energy, a rational response, uninvolved and objective in nature, concerned with self-preservation, planning, processing and making sense of things. FIVES over-emphasize their center, their natural style being to prefer observation to action, thinking to doing, collecting and organizing to getting involved in a hands-on experience. SEVENS underplay their center, their natural style being an optimistic preference to live in a dreamy future rather than in a pain-filled present. This they achieve by flitting from one interesting idea or plan to another, all the while radiating charm and good cheer. SIXES are very much out of touch with their center, their natural style being a law-abiding dependence on principles, rule-books or authority figures. In doing so they continually doubt their own judgment and forfeit their independence.

Defenses

It's worth remembering that our compulsion is essentially a negative, not a positive force. Although we regularly convince ourselves that there is a positive side to it, our compulsion is fundamentally destructive. It tears down rather than builds up. Deep down we know this to be true, so we devise strategies to keep it hidden from others and, more importantly, from ourselves. We avoid whatever we think might reveal what it is that basically makes us tick. Eventually we become so good at concealing what is going on that our compulsion becomes subconscious and, consequently, even more destructive.

The problem is compounded when the compulsion is further protected by means of a whole series of defense mechanisms designed specifically to protect the self-image we've constructed and which, at least in the first part of our life, appears to work for us. Our defense mechanisms can, of course, be very positive. They can help us cope in times of crisis, giving us the necessary breathing space to get our bearings and look for another way of coping with or adapting to unexpected problems. But when they enable us to distort and falsify reality they become destructive. When they prevent us from seeing who we really are they become quite harmful.

Very briefly we give here a run-down on the various compulsions, avoidances and defense mechanisms for each of the types. This may be helpful in locating our type, but the fact that many of us have been so successful in concealing our real self means that we may still be unwilling to own up to what has been going on.

As Perfectionists, ONES are doggedly determined that everything should be perfect. Unfortunately, as they see it from their own highly critical viewpoint, things are usually in a mess so they get angry and immediately want to clean it up or put it right. But, since anger is less than perfect, they reject it and try to avoid expressing it. Their basic defense mechanism is *reaction formation*—when confronted they will do the opposite of what is expected. This is basically a very clever way of pretending not to be angry while putting the knife in at the same time.

As Helpers, TWOS want to be of service. They take pride in helping everybody in need—except themselves. They think that having needs of their own is wrong, so they avoid any expression of their own neediness. Their basic defense mechanism is *repression*—a denial of their own dependence on others, to such an extent that they do not even admit the suggestion of it to be recognized by conscious awareness. This allows them to hold on to the illusion that they are strong, good-hearted people who take pride in being givers rather than takers.

As Achievers, THREES want to be efficient and to succeed. They want everything they do to be successful, so they avoid any connection with failure in case it tarnishes their polished image. Their basic defense mechanism is *identification*, which allows them to adapt to any situation, to change as befits the occasion, effectively to be whatever the other person wants them to be. This leads them to the point where they are both deceitfull ("economical with the truth") and completely out of touch with their own feelings.

As Artists, FOURS want to be authentic, one of a kind. They want everything to be so special that they avoid the ordinary and mundane as being beneath them and are envious of others who seem to radiate a certain *je ne sais quoi* (an indefinable something). Their basic defense mechanism is *introjection*, whereby they retreat into their rich inner world of fantasy and imagination rather than face the pain of the present. In doing so they identify with ideas or qualities from the outside world, projecting them on to their inner screen and making them their own. They also employ *artificial sublimination*, which involves them in an indirect expression of their feelings by way of artistic symbols, dramatic presentations or ritualized behavior. Having a poor self-image, FOURS hope that these defenses will prevent others from seeing them as they see themselves, and so will not reject them.

As Observers, FIVES are avaricious for knowledge. They soak up information from as wide a variety of sources as possible and process it to get the overall picture. This is to avoid meaninglessness—the emptiness inside brought on by the lack of rational explanation. Their basic defense mechanism is *withdrawal*, so that they adopt a non-involved approach to life. They also employ *compartmentalization*, which is a special form of withdrawal whereby they attempt to put various aspects of their lives into different drawers. By separating things into compartments FIVES are trying to limit interference in their own very ordered existence and to avoid the feeling of being overwhelmed.

As Supporters, SIXES look for their security in aligning themselves with authority, whether that comes in the form of people, institutions, books or laws. They are exceptionally loyal, but avoid originality because they are fundamentally fearful of "getting it wrong" and being accused of deviance and breaking the rules. Their defense mechanism is *projection*, whereby they screen worst possible scenarios in their minds, attributing their own hostile thoughts and negative ideas to others and then treating them with suspicion and mistrust before they have even had a chance to declare their position.

As Optimists, SEVENS are gluttons for happiness, which they can never get enough of. They continually look on the bright side of things and look for the silver lining to every cloud in their lives. They are determined to avoid the pain of being human and their defense mechanism is *rationalization*. This allows them to explain away problems or plan for all possible eventualities, so that as far as possible they will never be trapped in a situation which will cause them grief. It also means that they can generally come up with acceptable reasons to justify their addictive behavior.

As Leaders, EIGHTS have a lust for power. They are hooked on control and passionate in their pursuit of it. What they avoid like the plague is every sign of weakness. Their defense mechanism is both strong and simple—*denial*. In the battleground of life they seek to dominate and refuse to admit anything that might make them appear vulnerable, particularly when they are cornered or under duress.

As Mediators, NINES want peace and harmony at any price and are prepared to be slothfully inactive to get it. What they seek to avoid is any kind of conflict, so they "do nothing" to bring it about. Their defense mechanism is *narcotization*—they anesthetize the problem with a variety of painkillers ranging all the way from ice cream and television to substance abuse and other addictive behavior.

Wings

In terms of the Enneagram each person exemplifies one personality type. Within this type there is a whole range of possibilities, from being high up on the healthy, mature scale of the type to being low down on the unhealthy, immature scale. This in itself allows for a wide variation even within the same type. But the theory of the wings offers other sophisticated possibilities and allows us to distinguish still further between people.

There is no need to make a big issue out of this theory. Many teachers of the Enneagram reject it totally, others maintain that each type has only one wing, while some (including ourselves) still hang on to the theory of two wings because in their experience it appears to make sense. Without overcomplicating the issue, it can be summed up as follows.

The wings are the numbers on either side of an individual personality type. So, the SEVEN will have a wing in the SIX and a wing in the EIGHT. Generally speaking, in the early part of life we rely on the energy from one of our wings to help us mitigate the compulsiveness of our own personality type. Later in life it seems to be a help to people to balance out their compulsiveness with the help of their second, underused wing.

SEVENS, for example, are escapists. They want life to be a basically happy existence and they go out of their way to get out of painful situations. Their SIX wing helps keep them anchored and encourages them to remain loyal to friends or organizations even when the going gets tough. Their EIGHT wing enables them to endure the inevitable pain of life and face up to issues that need sorting out, in spite of the suffering which may be involved. Often, especially when we have not even begun our inner journey, we find that we are strongly influenced by one wing rather than another. Thus, a SEVEN with a dominant EIGHT wing will appear much different from a SEVEN with a strong SIX wing.

The real value of the wings, however, is that they allow us to step out of our own type for a while and see what life looks like through another pair of glasses. There are elements within the energies on either side of our own type which are familiar to us. This means we do not have to make a complete turn-around to see things from a different perspective. It also commences a process of freeing us from our fixated world view so that in time we can experience what it might be like to see life whole, from all the different viewpoints and not just from our own limited vision of what reality is or ought to be.

Arrows

The types on the Enneagram are connected by means of arrowed lines (note how the numbers are joined by the arrows in Figure 2). According to Enneagram theory, movement in the direction of the arrows is movement towards our stress point, which brings with it the prospect of increased immaturity and disintegration. Thus, the stress point for NINES is SIX, for SIXES is THREE, and for THREES is NINE. However, movement against the arrow is seen as movement towards integration and wholeness. When THREES take on the best energy of the SIX they are making positive strides towards maturity. We will be referring to this at the end of each of the personality profiles in Chapter 4 under the heading of *Conversion*.

For example, THREES are goal-orientated and do all they can to avoid failure. They are very competitive achievers and are prepared to jump ship before it goes down so as not to be associated with a disaster. When they move *against* their arrow (towards the best energy of the SIX) they find that maturity demands loyalty in times of difficulty. Thus they begin to learn to cooperate and stay with the project, accepting that commitment brings with it responsibilities. More importantly, their priorities change. They learn to value people more than projects and put relationships before achievements.

On the other hand, if they move *with* their arrow (towards the worst energy of the NINE), they will become even more out of touch with their feelings than they already are, and see no problem when their competitive spirit expresses itself in arrogant and manipulative behavior. If it should happen that they are unable to achieve their goals and allow themselves to take the easy way out, the emptiness and self-doubt of the negative energy of the NINES will intensify their feeling of failure, causing them to lose their sense of direction and either back off from a project or simply lose hope and just do nothing.

3

DISCOVERING YOUR TYPE

The following pages contain a series of statements which are directly related to the nine particular types on the Enneagram. They deal with gut, heart and head elements in each type, ranging from typical ways of behaving and feeling to characteristic attitudes.

It's important to remember that one personality type is not any better or any worse than another; they're just different, that's all. We cannot put one on a pedestal and throw stones at another.

Our identity is who we are. We cannot be someone else without sacrificing our own originality, without seriously damaging our special way of being in the world. Trying to live out of someone else's type is a mistake that some people make. It's like putting on a suit which is either two sizes too big or two sizes too small. It simply doesn't fit right. Our task in life is to learn to live in our own skin, inside our own heads, with our own heart pumping life into our own being.

To find your type it will help to proceed as follows:

■ Before you go through the statements, give a little consideration to what we said in the previous chapter on the *Centers* and *Defenses*. If you have already begun your inner journey it's possible that you will know your center, avoidance and defense mechanism, although it frequently comes as a surprise to people when they first discover what it is they are trying to keep hidden.

■ With that in mind, go through all the statements on the following pages, tick off those that apply to you and put a provisional total at the bottom as a guide. There is no need to ponder long over them. It's simply a matter of being completely honest with yourself and asking whether, given the normal pattern of your life, you agree or disagree with the statements. This is not a test where you must give the "correct" answer, so feel perfectly free to respond as you think appropriate. There is no need to keep looking over your shoulder to see what others might think if you tick off one statement and pass on another. Human respect has no place here.

■ If you're unsure of whether a statement applies to you or not, don't tick it off. If you think that by and large the statement applies to you, but not in every instance, consider it as a qualified yes and tick the box. It's worth noting that *how* we answer is as significant in telling us who we are as *what* we answer.

■ Don't worry if you find you can agree with many of the statements in each of the types. We all have elements of each type in our make-up. Some will be more plentiful than others. It is quite common for people to have 15 positive responses in one, 12 in another, 5 in a third, and so on. But when you have gone through all nine sets of statements you will be in a better position to judge which type is likely to be yours. One of the advantages of going through all the types is to see our relative strengths and weaknesses, to learn what elements we have in common with other types, and what areas we need to work on. It can also indicate which of our wings is currently dominant and which is underdeveloped.

■ When going through the statements there is no need to consider motivation, merely whether you agree or disagree. But keep in mind that it will be the compulsive pattern, which drives you to behave in one way rather than another, that will finally determine what type you are. So, for example, if you are inclined to be a workaholic, you could be a ONE or a THREE. As you will learn from the special profiles in the next chapter, ONES work hard to get things right; they show a dogged persistence in this so that work drains their energy. They are rather like the *domestiques* in cycling, who do all the hard slog and donkey work, but who do not have the energy at the end to shine as winners. The THREES, on the other hand, work in order to succeed, to avoid failure. They find energy in their work; it exhilarates them. Unlike the ONES, they are not exhausted at the end. It all seems to come easily to them, so much so that you can almost see them in the yellow jersey during the stages of the *Tour de France*, sprinting ahead of the *domestiques* at the end of a long day's ride, hands held high, the image of success.

When you have gone through the nine sets of statements, check the totals. If you have ticked off 20-25 statements in one particular set, it is entirely possible that you belong to that type. However, it may not be as clear-cut as all that, so it will help if you read the personality profiles outlined in the next chapter. Having done so, go through your checklist again and see whether this time around your type becomes any clearer.

■ If you are embarrassed to find that you are a particular type, this is actually a good sign. It means that you have understood that the Enneagram is about identifying your hidden compulsion and then opening yourself to the process of conversion. It also means that you have not fallen into the trap of mistaking your own type for what might appear at first glance to be a more "attractive" one. The fact is that each type has its dark side and core sin. So, we don't have to like our type, but we do have to identify it.

■ If you are still unsure of your type, don't worry. It sometimes takes a while for everything to fall into place. Meanwhile, it might help to ask a relative, spouse, friend or colleague who knows you well to go through the process and see which type they think is most typical of you. It's interesting how others can sometimes put their finger on our compulsion quicker than we can ourselves. Distance lends a certain objectivity to their assessment and so can reveal aspects which we are unable to recognize. But beware of the possibility that they are not as perceptive as they think, and are merely reflecting back to you the self-image you have successfully managed to present to them. One of the benefits of doing a workshop is that you can discuss the results with someone who is experienced in looking at the patterns and who will, therefore, be able to offer useful guidance. But at the end of the day it all comes down to your own personal self-discovery.

■ Whatever the result of this self-administered assessment, consider it as provisional, not etched in metal. Like all profiles, there is still another side to be seen. Given time, the whole face will be illuminated. For the present, stay with what you have learned about yourself and don't minimize the insights which have been obtained. Discovering what makes us tick can be a profoundly enlightening experience. It can help us see aspects of our character that we had previously neglected and can go a long way towards helping us come to terms with ourselves and others.

ONES

☐ 1. I like everything to be as perfect as possible.
☐ 2. I work very hard to get rid of my faults.
☐ 3. I find I apologize a lot for all sorts of things.
☐ 4. The adjective which describes me best is probably "finicky."
☐ 5. It upsets me enormously when people aren't fair.
☐ 6. I always think I'm not good enough to merit other people's love.
☐ 7. I find it difficult to relax and take time out.
☐ 8. I have an in-built conscience which continually nags at me.
☐ 9. I identify with reformers and all those who fight for what's right.
☐ 10. Finding the least flaw in something puts me off.
☐ 11. I see things in terms of black or white rather than as shades of grey.
☐ 12. I rarely have enough time in which to do everything I need to do.
☐ 13. I get upset when things aren't the way they should be.
☐ 14. I'm a worrier.
☐ 15. I like to be right; I don't like to be wrong.
☐ 16. I resent it when people don't measure up to what they should be.
☐ 17. I can be very strict and puritanical at times.
☐ 18. I pay too much attention to details and minutiae.
☐ 19. I'm always finding fault and noticing what's missing.
☐ 20. When things go wrong I keep analyzing precisely why.
☐ 21. I feel everyone should be honest, myself most of all.
☐ 22. I object strongly to wasting time.
☐ 23. I'm continually blaming myself for not being better.
☐ 24. I'm generally restless, striving continuously for what's beyond my grasp.
☐ 25. I am very resentful, sometimes unbearably so.

TWOS

☐ 1.   I feel I'm always the one who's reaching out and giving.

☐ 2.   Helping comes naturally to me.

☐ 3.   People can get close to me.

☐ 4.   I often feel empty inside.

☐ 5.   I have the feeling that I'm not appreciated most of the time.

☐ 6.   I'm the counsellor, advice-giver and sympathizer all rolled into one.

☐ 7.   Being needed is important to me.

☐ 8.   I can always be counted on to come to the rescue in a crisis.

☐ 9.   Even my free time is given over to others.

☐ 10   Caring is my one big preoccupation.

☐ 11   I like to think I'm self-sufficient.

☐ 12.   I'm a flatterer.

☐ 13.   I'd much rather give than receive.

☐ 14.   It's possible that others think I'm very emotional.

☐ 15.   Sometimes other people just "use" me, and it gets to me.

☐ 16.   I prefer not to dwell on my own needs and wants.

☐ 17.   If I'm honest, I know I have a "martyr complex."

☐ 18.   I feel good about myself when I help meet others' needs.

☐ 19.   I'm proud of my service to others.

☐ 20.   I resent my time being taken from me.

☐ 21.   I don't get openly angry, but I do tend to manipulate.

☐ 22.   I can become quite aggressive when people go against me.

☐ 23.   My own needs are secondary to those of others.

☐ 24.   People aren't always grateful for the trouble I take on their behalf.

☐ 25.   I like to compliment people.

THREES

☐ 1.   I move in the fast lane.

☐ 2.   I'm a natural when it comes to plans and organization.

☐ 3.   I like to know where I fit in and what's expected of me.

☐ 4.   I am an excellent team worker.

☐ 5.   My image is important to me; I like others to see me as a success.

☐ 6.   I can lose my identity when over-involved with work.

☐ 7.   I live and breathe "success."

☐ 8.   Plans can be more important than people.

☐ 9.   I don't mind boasting about what I've done or who I've seen, etc.

☐ 10   I'm a quick and efficient worker and am often envied in this regard.

☐ 11   I like to keep tabs on the progress I've made.

☐ 12.   Failure is to be avoided at all costs.

☐ 13.   I find I neglect my inner world.

☐ 14.   I often have to compromise in order to get others to come with me.

☐ 15.   I have no difficulty in decision making.

☐ 16.   I think you need to be successful for others to take notice of you.

☐ 17.   I am perfectly capable of bending the truth to suit my purposes.

☐ 18.   I can be quite aggressive, especially with people who fail.

☐ 19.   I tend to feel inferior if I'm not on top.

☐ 20.   I like starting projects and then passing them on to others to finish.

☐ 21.   I project a good image; I'd be great in advertising.

☐ 22.   I know what I want and I set out to get it.

☐ 23.   People mightn't believe it, but I do suffer from a fair bit of anxiety.

☐ 24.   I'm very impressed by those who have achieved a lot in their lives.

☐ 25.   I emphasize the positive and try not to remember my failures.

FOURS

- [ ] 1. I genuinely feel quite special.
- [ ] 2. Experiences go deeper with me than with most.
- [ ] 3. I tend to do things with panache and style.
- [ ] 4. I sometimes feel I'm locked in my past.
- [ ] 5. The symbolic in life attracts me.
- [ ] 6. I am often taken up with thoughts of loss, pain and death.
- [ ] 7. I find an emotional outlet in dramatic presentation or expression.
- [ ] 8. My mood swings from very high to very low; in between is dull.
- [ ] 9. People feel I look down on them and am somehow snobbish.
- [ ] 10. I am no stranger to depression.
- [ ] 11. I often seem to whine about what's going wrong in my life.
- [ ] 12. I frequently wish I had others' gifts and talents.
- [ ] 13. Anything that offends good taste offends me.
- [ ] 14. I am often misunderstood.
- [ ] 15. I like to surround myself with beautiful things.
- [ ] 16. I empathize so deeply with others that I can really feel their hurt.
- [ ] 17. Life is tough, but I try to smile away the tears.
- [ ] 18. I rarely think of myself as being ordinary.
- [ ] 19. I tend to avoid fuss in my dress.
- [ ] 20. I don't seem to be as happy as others are.
- [ ] 21. Many people are just not able to understand how I feel.
- [ ] 22. I'm more upset than most about the ending of relationships.
- [ ] 23. People think of me as being over-dramatic.
- [ ] 24. I often wonder if I react to situations with enough depth of feeling.
- [ ] 25. I appreciate most art forms and consider myself artistic.

FIVES

☐ 1. I'm often an observer rather than a participant.
☐ 2. I don't like sharing my feelings.
☐ 3. I need a lot of time to myself.
☐ 4. Giving comes hard to me. I prefer to accept, take and receive.
☐ 5. I tend to hoard what I know, because knowledge is precious.
☐ 6. I'm stingy with my time, and frugal with money.
☐ 7. I'm good at getting a detached overview of complex problems.
☐ 8. My motto for problem solving is to "think things through."
☐ 9. I work best on my own.
☐ 10. Deep down, I'm scared of being empty.
☐ 11. I don't like to shout. It annoys me when I'm told to speak up.
☐ 12. I find it difficult to ask people to help me.
☐ 13. I dislike being short-changed in anything. I like value for money.
☐ 14. I'm not the pushy type.
☐ 15. I question everything to find out how things operate.
☐ 16. I rarely "sugar the pill"; I sometimes lack tact.
☐ 17. I give the appearance of being cool, detached and above it all.
☐ 18. I mutter words like "dope," "nitwit," "stupid," "fool" when upset.
☐ 19. I'm happy to let others start the ball rolling.
☐ 20. I'm a magpie, picking up things which just might come in useful.
☐ 21. I find small talk difficult and can clam up in company.
☐ 22. The grand design is more important to me than the concrete details.
☐ 23. I tend to think issues through before discussing them.
☐ 24. I don't speak as much as others, so my views have to be asked for.
☐ 25. I'm non-plussed when asked to express my feelings.

SIXES

☐ 1. I'm generally balanced in my views.
☐ 2. I make very few spontaneous decisions.
☐ 3. Loyalty to the group is very important to me.
☐ 4. I am sensitive, "touchy," and I don't like being crossed.
☐ 5. I often sacrifice my independence for security.
☐ 6. Fear looms large in my life.
☐ 7. I like knowing what is expected of me.
☐ 8. I take sides in an argument and always want to know who is on my side.
☐ 9. Without rules there's no knowing what people would get up to.
☐ 10. I'm often riddled with doubt.
☐ 11. I feel I'm a coward at times.
☐ 12. I'm quicker than most at spotting trouble and danger.
☐ 13. My sense of duty often determines what I do or don't do.
☐ 14. I like to explore all the possibilities before taking action.
☐ 15. I support authority rather than go against it.
☐ 16. I come across to others as being a bit dogmatic.
☐ 17. I'm shy.
☐ 18. I often change my mind.
☐ 19. I'm often unaware of how direct I am, though I see it in others.
☐ 20. I am overly serious.
☐ 21. Indecision prevents me from achieving much good.
☐ 22. I feel inhibited in many ways.
☐ 23. I envy those who can make quick decisions.
☐ 24. I prefer to stick to a timetable than to let things just happen.
☐ 25. I find I'm probably more defensive than most people.

SEVENS

☐ 1. Most people are too serious; if you lighten up you brighten up.

☐ 2. I want people to think of me as a fun person to be with.

☐ 3. I've rarely met a person I couldn't like.

☐ 4. I love to daydream.

☐ 5. I'm a good conversationalist, with a fund of stories to tell.

☐ 6. I try to avoid painful situations; if I'm hurt, I withdraw.

☐ 7. You can never have too much of a good thing.

☐ 8. I'm often complimented on being the life and soul of the party.

☐ 9. I'm very open to people—not suspicious or judgmental.

☐ 10. I was very happy as a child.

☐ 11. I like to get a quick response to requests; I hate waiting around.

☐ 12. I make great plans.

☐ 13. I'm much too optimistic a person to dwell on life's difficulties.

☐ 14. I'm very much a child at heart, playful and fun-loving.

☐ 15. I prefer my conversation light and cheerful, not serious and heavy.

☐ 16. I enjoy life to the full.

☐ 17. In spite of the hassle, things generally work out in the end.

☐ 18. Everything has its place in the grand design of the universe.

☐ 19. It's morbid to be sad for too long.

☐ 20. My plans are often a bit up in the air and short on concrete details.

☐ 21. I don't have the perseverance to match my enthusiasms.

☐ 22. People see me as superficial rather than substantial.

☐ 23. In my view the future holds great things in store for us.

☐ 24. I like things to be nice and pleasant.

☐ 25. I don't like confrontations; I prefer to paper over the cracks.

EIGHTS

☐ 1. I believe if you want something you should fight for it.

☐ 2. People don't scare me; if they need to be tackled, no problem.

☐ 3. I find it hard when I'm told I have to change.

☐ 4. People bring their problems on themselves.

☐ 5. I'm hard on people who hurt me and often punish them for it.

☐ 6. My initial response to requests is "no"; it gives me time to analyze.

☐ 7. I'm a bit of a rebel; I don't always conform.

☐ 8. I'm a hard worker.

☐ 9. I enjoy power and using it.

☐ 10. I'm a bit coarse and crude at times; "earthy" in the best sense.

☐ 11. If I am not satisfied I say so and make no bones about it.

☐ 12. In a group I always know who has the power and who has not.

☐ 13. I make decisions quickly, sometimes without having the full facts.

☐ 14. If things don't move along I soon get bored.

☐ 15. I'm not slow to exploit other's vulnerable points if necessary.

☐ 16. I can't "let sleeping dogs lie."

☐ 17. I'm very protective of those in my care.

☐ 18. I'm very strong on justice; injustice is unacceptable to me.

☐ 19. Introspection is frequently just a cop-out from action.

☐ 20. I'm a forceful person; a good adjective would be "aggressive."

☐ 21. I can make things happen and get projects finished.

☐ 22. I have a sensitive and tender side which I find hard to express.

☐ 23. I find it difficult to listen.

☐ 24. I am rough and abrasive, and can grind others down.

☐ 25. I find it difficult to trust myself.

NINES

☐ 1. People see me as relaxed; a good adjective would be "easy-going."

☐ 2. It's pointless getting too upset about things.

☐ 3. I try to pour oil on troubled waters by minimizing the problems.

☐ 4. I need a push to get started.

☐ 5. I have a great inner peace.

☐ 6. One of my great gifts is that I'm balanced and stable.

☐ 7. "Mañana" (tomorrow) is a lovely word; things can always wait.

☐ 8. I generally take the easy way out.

☐ 9. I usually sleep very well.

☐ 10. "Let nothing disturb you" is a good motto.

☐ 11. Change upsets me a lot, and I'm difficult to move.

☐ 12. I really don't see myself as being very important.

☐ 13. I don't often get too excited or enthusiastic about things.

☐ 14. I tend to repress my feelings.

☐ 15. I often give the appearance of being drained of energy.

☐ 16. I am often indecisive, not wanting to say "yes" or "no."

☐ 17. I do all I can to preserve my energy.

☐ 18. I see myself as a mediator and a peacemaker.

☐ 19. I am not very punctual.

☐ 20. I like to have time to myself to just sit and do nothing.

☐ 21. My attention wanders a bit, so listening is difficult for me.

☐ 22. Never stand when you can sit, or sit when you can lie down!

☐ 23. In general I resign myself to the way things are.

☐ 24. I tend to be forgetful.

☐ 25. When you come right down to it, people don't differ all that much.

4

PERSONALITY PROFILES

The profiles outlined in this chapter all follow a similar pattern and should be a help to you in discovering your personality type. Each one begins with an Identity Card, which gives a quick overview of the type from the following perspectives:

Name: This refers to the name we use in this book for the personality type. It's our attempt to encapsulate the central energy of the type into a single word. However, we're aware that this is not always completely successful and that other authors prefer different names. What is important is to understand the personality referred to by the name.

Identity: This refers to how each one of us perceives ourselves to be, not necessarily who we are in reality. The statement of identity which each type makes comes directly from their compulsive view of the world. It is, therefore, a very personal summing up and is not to be mistaken for an objective assessment.

Center: This refers to the preferred basic energy (gut, heart or head) out of which the personality type operates. It was more fully discussed in Chapter 2.

Compulsion: This refers to the central fixation or motivating force which drives us to do what we do. The less we are aware of it, the more powerful it is in directing our way of being in the world, and the more difficult it is to control, particularly in situations of stress.

Passion: This refers to the particular vice or capital sin to which we are most susceptible and which we must deal with if we are to become spiritually whole. Christian theologians have traditionally listed seven such as capital or radical sins: pride, avarice, lust, anger, gluttony, envy, and sloth. The Enneagram, however, helps us to identify two more which are particularly appropriate to our own times—deceit and fear. All nine passions are singularly effective in preventing us from accepting God's love in our lives. The one to which we are especially prone is, for us, our root sin (see Figure 4 for a schematic diagram indicating the vices and the corresponding virtues for each of the Enneagram types).

Outlet: Consciously or unconsciously we generally seek to hide our predominant vice, but one way or another it will surface. Our outlet is the way in which our passion surfaces. An example would be the anger which the ONES try so hard to conceal, even from themselves, but which comes out in various ways as resentment. Our outlet is, therefore, like a safety valve which allows our vice to surface in more or less tolerable ways.

Fear: This refers to what we avoid most in our lives. It is intimately bound up with our compulsion. THREES, for instance, fear failure because it is the opposite of the success which they continually crave.

Rejection: This refers to what we deny or overlook in our lives because it would damage our self-image. It is part and parcel of both our compulsion and our fear. TWOS, for example, reject their own needs because they mistakenly believe that those who help others cannot be seen to have needs themselves.

Defense: This refers to the strategy we employ to defend our self-image and conceal our compulsion. Our characteristic psychological defense mechanism is most obviously employed in situations of stress. There was a fuller discussion and definition of the various defense mechanisms in Chapter 2.

Focus: This refers to the central issues on which we concentrate or the particular way we pay attention to these issues. What we focus on helps reveal our hidden compulsive energy.

Stance: This refers to two elements: (a) how we see ourselves in relation to the world and (b) what our normal preferred way of acting is likely to be.

(a) There are three basic ways in which we look at ourselves in relation to the world. We can consider ourselves to be *bigger* than the world; in other words, we feel confident and well able to cope with whatever life holds in store for us. We can consider ourselves to be *smaller* than the world; in other words, we feel unsure and see ourselves as always having to fight hard to get things done. Or we can consider ourselves as having to *adjust* to the world; in other words, we have to conform so as to be able to achieve our goal.

(b) There are also three ways in which we prefer to act, depending on our particular type. We can be *aggressive*, or essentially hostile in our behavior; we can be *dependent*, or essentially relational in our behavior; or we can be *withdrawing*, so that whenever possible we remove ourselves and do not engage with life.

The differing personalty types will have different combinations of these elements as indicated in the Identity Cards for each type.

Need: This refers to our most fundamental psychological need—that element which will help us defuse our compulsive energy and grow to psychological maturity. Thus, the basic need of the FIVES, who live primarily in their heads, is to get involved in the nitty-gritty aspects of life (see Figure 3 for an overview of the things we compulsively want in life and, by contrast, what we need most to grow to wholeness).

Healing: This refers to our most fundamental spiritual need—that spiritual gift which we need to foster in order to remain open to growth in holiness. So, for SIXES, this will mean trusting in God as the ultimate support in their lives.

Virtue: This refers to the form of goodness or moral excellence which is best exemplified by a particular personality when it is not locked into its compulsive world view. As will be seen from Figure 4, it is the opposite of the characteristic vice of each of the personalities. The virtue of the SEVENS is temperance, their typical vice being gluttony.

In addition to the Identity Card, each personality profile which follows has a section on the childhood origins of their fixated world view, a summary of their compulsion, and pointers which help each individual to minimize the impact of this compulsion and so move towards conversion. The movement towards conversion was discussed in Chapter 2 under the heading of *Arrows.*

ONES

IDENTITY CARD

NAME:	Perfectionist
IDENTITY:	I'm right and hard-working
CENTER:	Gut
COMPULSION:	Perfection
PASSION:	Anger
OUTLET:	Resentment
FEAR:	Imperfection
REJECTION:	Direct anger
DEFENSE:	Reaction formation
FOCUS:	Rules and criticism
STANCE:	Smaller/Aggressive
NEED:	To relax
HEALING:	Growth
VIRTUE:	Serenity

Childhood

ONES have lived all their lives with the expectations of others. The central message they receive as children is to work hard, be perfect and not be a "bad" little child. They quickly learn what the rules are and try hard to put them into practice. By doing so they think their parents and other significant adults will love them. At the very least they will be complimented and given approval. With these rules they have a standard by which to judge others and know where they stand in any relationships they make. Criticism from parents can lead them to develop a negative self-image, become resentful and humorless, finding fault with everything.

Compulsion

ONES can be good conversationalists and charming companions. But their obsession with perfection can make others feel uncomfortable in their presence. They are very orderly and meticulous. They are always on time. They work hard and methodically, and are frequently workaholics.

They avoid anger, deny its existence in them and, as far as possible, keep their hostility in check. But it generally comes out as resentment, and is evident in the edginess of their speech and behavior.

They feel they have to be right and to put others straight. In doing so, they are often intolerant, self-righteous and frequently make mountains out of molehills. Nothing is ever good enough—not even themselves. They are compelled to clean up the mess and impose order on what they see as chaos. They are sticklers for detail, checking and double-checking to make sure everything is correct, and frequently getting so bogged down in minutiae that they fail to see the woods for the trees.

They have a strong inner critical voice. They are generally rather uptight and serious, continually trying to keep their emotions in control. There is never enough time in the day for them, and they become frustrated and even depressed when pressurized too much. They are very impatient and carry a "hit list" of frustrations. They tend to be stubborn in getting their own way. They are often very tense and it is difficult for them to relax. They are compulsive about trying to meet all the demands others make on them, because only then do they feel they are loved.

Careers which suit their concern for rules and perfection include the law, the army, teaching, accountancy and medicine.

Further Comments:

_____

_____

_____

_____

_____

_____

_____

_____

Conversion

To achieve integration ONES need to take on the best aspects of the SEVEN. This will help them to:

•*Relax and take things easy.* They are prone to take themselves too seriously and to overwork. They need to "lighten up," take part in fun and games, and accept that this is good.

•*Experience their anger.* They need to own their anger, while recognizing that they do not have to act out of it.

•*Get in touch with their feelings,* especially the ones they are least happy with—the messy, chaotic and inappropriate ones which they seek to control. People are not condemned for having limitations. Indeed, true love means being accepted, faults and all.

•*Stop judging themselves and others* by their hidden book of rules. They need to be less rigid and more patient.

•*Appreciate the principle of growth.* Mistakes are a normal part of the way people grow to maturity. This is a process which takes time and cannot be rushed.

TWOS

IDENTITY CARD

NAME:	Helper
IDENTITY:	I'm caring
CENTER:	Heart
COMPULSION:	Service
PASSION:	Pride
OUTLET:	Flattery
FEAR:	Being useless
REJECTION:	Own needs
DEFENSE:	Repression
FOCUS:	Empathy and Adapting
STANCE:	Bigger/Dependent
NEED:	To accept real worth
HEALING:	Gift/Grace
VIRTUE:	Humility

Childhood

TWOS are always ready to help their parents with little tasks about the house. They are thoughtful and conscientious, see what needs to be done and do it. They light up when praised for this, and are ready to do more. They are sensitive to others' feelings, and are prepared to sacrifice their own to please others. Consequently they are always welcome and well liked. This has always been the central demand made on them—to please others, to put others before self, not to contradict or disagree with whoever is in charge. As children TWOS quickly sense what others need, adapt themselves to meet these needs, and so gain approval and notice.

Compulsion

TWOS are warm, sensitive and helpful people. They are capable of empathizing very well with the feelings of others, and of expressing emotion easily. The problem for them is that these feelings generally relate to others, rarely to themselves. They repress their own emotions and, while giving generously to others, deny that they have needs themselves. They get their identity from helping others, so that sometimes their service is less a concern for others than a way of being personally alive. They often have a "me first" attitude.

They look for attention by responding to the real or imagined needs of others. To get this they can be manipulative. They rarely ask for favors directly. They expect others to notice what they need without having to be asked. If the other still does not notice and they badly need something, they will flatter and manipulate to get what they want. When they are rejected in any way they adopt their martyr complex and become victims.

Since their greatest need is to be loved, they are also prone to infatuation. They are warm, caring people who love to touch and reach out to others. But they are so busy meeting the needs of others that they become out of touch with their own. Although their attention and warmth promise friendship, they find closeness and intimacy difficult. Their seductiveness and charm are meant not for real intimacy but for admiration and approval. Very compulsive TWOS can become hysterics—prone to over-dramatize, exhibitionism and exaggerated language.

Careers that attract TWOS are teaching, nursing, ministry, social service.

Further Comments

_____

_____

_____

_____

_____

_____

_____

_____

_____

_____

_____

_____

_____

_____

_____

_____

_____

_____

_____

_____

_____

_____

Conversion

To achieve integration TWOS need to take on the best aspects of the FOUR. This will help them to:

• *Get in touch with their own feelings and needs,* so that they can accept themselves as they really are. They are bad at recognizing their own needs and must own this and change it.

• *Learn that love cannot be bought or earned.* Therefore they must curb their tendency to call attention to themselves by reminding others of the good they have done for them. This is always seen for what it is—an attempt to "buy" affection.

• *Know that they are lovable for who they are.* Unwillingness to change is grounded for them in the fear of not being loved. Their identity is so bound up with what others think of them that any change will take time.

• *Appreciate their real worth* and understand that they do not have to gain approval by being either helpful or helpless. Their goal is partnership, not manipulation.

• *Help others without ulterior motives.* They must not expect favors or expressions of gratitude for what they have done.

THREES

IDENTITY CARD

NAME:	Achiever
IDENTITY:	I'm successful
CENTER:	Heart
COMPULSION:	Efficiency
PASSION:	Deceit
OUTLET:	Vanity
FEAR:	Failure
REJECTION:	Lying
DEFENSE:	Identification
FOCUS:	Image and Performance
STANCE:	Adjust/Aggressive
NEED:	Examine the Image
HEALING:	Depend on God's Will
VIRTUE:	Truth

Childhood

THREES are busy and competitive little bees as children. They need to be, because all too often what they do is just not good enough for the significant adults in their lives. Performance is everything, they are told, so they try to make their parents proud of them by doing whatever it takes. Success and achievement are vital to them, because otherwise they feel they can neither be loved nor accepted. So they quickly find the things they are good at and which will get them attention. These they pursue, often to the neglect of their feelings and emotions. If not careful they can lose their sense of personal identity through over-identification with their role.

Compulsion

The enthusiasm of the THREES makes them very attractive and the fact that they get things done means they are very much in demand. They are full of energy, creative, competitive and very productive. They are frequently referred to as being "bright-eyed and bushy-tailed." But their need to be successful and to be seen as such can lead them to neglect their feelings, become exploitative and opportunistic, and to bend the truth to their own needs. They are "image makers" who prefer to dwell on the successful elements of their projects rather than on their drawbacks or even failures.

THREES are frequently workaholics. They revel in activity and can become hard taskmasters, being particularly dismissive of inefficiency, time-wasting and incompetence. They like to be in charge of projects but do not acknowledge other people's contributions to their success. If a project is likely to sink they make certain that they don't sink with it.

They wear a mask without knowing it is there. This extends to their feelings which they have learned to turn on to order. They feel what they are supposed to feel at the appropriate times. They are not comfortable revealing their feelings and avoid it by diverting attention to some interesting activity. Real intimacy is a problem for them and to avoid difficulties they give it a low priority. Action takes precedence over emotion for them, so they often seem distant and superficial.

THREES are good conversationalists, regularly telling people what will please them or impress them. Since their image is all important, they dress well and for success. They have a very busy social life. They court popularity and love being in the public eye. A corollary to this is that they have no real sense of privacy—for themselves or others.

Given their talents they make excellent managers, administrators, and media/advertising executives.

Further Comments

_____

_____

_____

_____

_____

Conversion

To achieve integration THREES need to take on the best aspects of the SIX. This will help them to:

•*Confront their deceptions.* They are great self-deceivers and need to learn that appearances are not everything.

•*Develop the virtues of truthfulness and honesty.* This involves not bragging about their achievements, or exaggerating their importance so as to impress others.

•*Slow down and take stock of their lives,* especially their relationships, activities, emotions and values. They need to accept that they are loved for who they are rather than for what they accomplish.

•*Own and accept failures.* Only an inflated ego needs continual success. Being human makes them more desirable.

•*Cooperate rather than compete with others.* There is no need to hog the limelight, put others down or make them feel inferior. They need to take the feelings of others into account.

FOURS

IDENTITY CARD

NAME:	Artist
IDENTITY:	I'm unique and intuitive
CENTER:	Heart
COMPULSION:	Authenticity
PASSION:	Envy
OUTLET:	Melancholy
FEAR:	Ordinary
REJECTION:	Mundane
DEFENSE:	Introjection
FOCUS:	Intense and Unavailable
STANCE:	Smaller/Withdrawing
NEED:	Sense of present reality
HEALING:	Union with God
VIRTUE:	Equanimity

Childhood

The FOURS see themselves as tragic figures, very different from everybody else. As children they may have lost a parent, been abandoned or felt abandoned. The joy in their lives is therefore brief, because they expect to be let down, disappointed and hurt. This personal sadness makes them so special that they think nobody else can understand their pain or loneliness. They learned the hard way that they couldn't count on their parents or other significant adults to be there when needed, either to comfort or support them. So they adopt the policy of rejecting others before they are rejected. They try to avoid emotional involvement, making up for it with a rich, symbolic fantasy life.

Compulsion

The FOURS see themselves as special and are very sensitive to beauty in all its manifestations. They can be quite artistic and rely on imagery and symbols to describe their feelings and experiences. Nothing is ordinary in their lives. They have no time for the mundane or commonplace. Since even their joys and sorrows are either dramatic or tragic, they don't believe anyone else can experience life at their kind of depth. In this sense they can be emotional snobs, sometimes even being contemptuous or disdainful of the feelings of others. They see their attraction to beauty and their artistic good sense as compensating for their lack of self-esteem. They have style and dress accordingly.

Their imagination is very active and they like ritual and drama. They are often theatrical in their responses, frequently rehearsing conversations in their head before having them. In this sense, even though they desire spontaneity, they never achieve it. They imagine that if they were simple, down-to-earth individuals people would no longer love them or relate to them. Their fear that others will not understand them, and so will leave them alone, means that they get melancholic and sad. Indeed, they often seem to need to be mournful in order to feel alive. They analyze things to death, continually dwell on the past, and are subject to moodiness and depression. They are always attracted to what is outside their grasp, and never satisfied when it is theirs. They envy the fact that other people seem to possess what they lack. Manners, etiquette and good taste are important to them. They may clam up at times and harbor their negative feelings, but, like an oyster, they can also produce a pearl from a piece of grit.

FOURS tend to be actors, writers, musicians, poets and artists.

Further Comments

_____

_____

_____

_____

_____

Conversion

To achieve integration FOURS need to take on the best aspects of the ONE. This will help them to:

•*Live in the present with all its troubles.* If they are ever to become happy and content they cannot remain fixed in idealizations and flights of fantasy.

• *Stop envying others and making comparisons.* It will help them if they can see both the positive and negative elements in the things that happen.

• *Accept that the self is not identical with feelings.* In particular, the presence of negative feelings does not mean the absence of positive ones.

• *Use their talents productively,* no matter how insignificant their efforts may seem. They must not wait until they are in the mood but become active in the world as it is.

• *Avoid rehearsing everything in their imagination,* especially when it involves over-romantic or negative feelings.

FIVES

IDENTITY CARD

NAME:	Observer
IDENTITY:	I'm perceptive
CENTER:	Head
COMPULSION:	Knowledge
PASSION:	Avarice
OUTLET:	Stinginess
FEAR:	Emptiness
REJECTION:	Meaninglessness
DEFENSE:	Withdrawal
FOCUS:	Observation and Theories
STANCE:	Bigger/Withdrawing
NEED:	To get involved
HEALING:	Divine Providence
VIRTUE:	Detachment

Childhood

Children who are FIVES are generally as quiet as mice. They retreat into themselves and keep their own counsel. But they also keep a close eye on what is going on around them. Often they play at being invisible so as not to attract attention. They perceive parents as overly intrusive, sometimes to the point where they seem to know what is going on even in the child's mind. They are not encouraged to become emotionally close. The family may have moved house often. FIVES learn to cope by pursuing privacy and living in the world of the mind. They read a lot but don't share their thoughts with others unless they have to. They know what's happening but protect themselves from involvement by getting lost in the crowd.

Compulsion

FIVES have a great gift for getting to the heart of the matter and seeing the overall picture. The problem is that they find it very difficult to commit themselves and get involved. They are observers rather than participants. It is difficult to get to know them because they only give so much of themselves. They compartmentalize their lives. They are very private and do not like their physical or mental space invaded. This gives them a detached and somewhat impersonal air.

Emotions are secondary to the FIVES. They isolate their feelings in order to give them time to come to a decision. If they are asked about their feelings they often talk about what they think. They are uncomfortable and sometimes embarrassed at parties, not having much skill at small talk. They frequently forget names and give the impression of being stingy with their time and money. But, when they are interested, they can be very good listeners and, since they are eager to know everything they can, they are usually open, receptive and non-judgmental.

They pursue knowledge to fill their inner emptiness. They never tell you everything they know, in case it drains their resources. Moreover, they rarely think they have much that is worth saying—their knowledge is never sufficiently complete and comprehensive to warrant it. Hence they can find themselves taking endless courses in order to increase their store of knowledge and to avoid getting involved in the nuts and bolts of day-to-day activity. They are forever preparing themselves. Since they generally desire anonymity, preferring to blend in rather than stand out, they are not seen as a threat, yet they can be both profound and provocative.

Given their talents they make good hermits, researchers, interviewers, librarians and counsellors.

Further Comments

_____

_____

_____

_____

_____

_____
_____
_____
_____
_____
_____
_____
_____
_____
_____
_____
_____
_____
_____
_____
_____
_____
_____
_____

Conversion
To achieve integration FIVES need to take on the best aspects
of the EIGHT. This will help them to:

•*Become involved and committed.* They need to become active
and "doers," not just observers or theoreticians.

•*Share more of themselves.* To counterbalance their avarice
and possessiveness they need to risk self-disclosure and share
more in terms of time, knowledge and money.

•*Recognize that emotions, too, give insight.* Self-knowledge is
not limited to theories and analysis.

•*Trust others and cooperate more.* This will help open them up
emotionally and allow them to experience companionship.

•*Avoid jumping to conclusions.* Theorizing at the drop of a hat
can contribute to poor judgment. Though it may be difficult
for them, they should consult someone whose judgment they
respect.

SIXES

IDENTITY CARD

NAME:	Supporter
IDENTITY:	I'm loyal
CENTER:	Head
COMPULSION:	Security
PASSION:	Fear/Doubt
OUTLET:	Cowardice
FEAR:	Fear
REJECTION:	Originality
DEFENSE:	Projection
FOCUS:	Danger and Authority
STANCE:	Adjust/Dependent
NEED:	Faith/Courage
HEALING:	Trust in God
VIRTUE:	Courage

Childhood

SIXES go through childhood with antennae on permanent alert. They have a highly developed sense of danger and grow up experiencing a great deal of fear. The ten commandments may have been drummed into them, with the emphasis on all the *Don'ts* They may even have been threatened with the "Boogie Man." As a result, they quickly learn to be cautious, careful, wary and suspicious. Not having received much encouragement to succeed they develop a low self-esteem. They respond to the threat of danger in two basic ways. The first is to avoid it by becoming very obedient, conformist and conscientious. The second is to face and attempt to defuse it. This can sometimes lead to anger which expresses itself in delinquent behavior.

Compulsion

Because of their early experiences, SIXES are plagued by both fear and doubt about themselves and others. They are so cautious that they have great difficulty in making decisions. They see all the possible snags and these inhibit their action. They much prefer to be told what they do by someone in a position of authority rather than risk making decisions themselves. They are, therefore, very good party people, loyal to whatever group they have joined, obeying the rules and keen to ensure that others do the same. They like the sense of solidarity and support which belonging to a group brings. Though sometimes they think the group demands too much of them, they also find it hard to tolerate it when others buck the system with apparent impunity. When they themselves deviate from the rules, they can't admit it and use denial and projection to cover their shame. They tend to spot the mote in someone else's eye while overlooking the beam in their own.

It is important for SIXES to know who belongs and who does not. Equally important is their precise rank and power within the group. They are generally mistrustful of anyone purporting to help them, and are quick to notice interlopers with hidden agendas. They do not like it when others question their opinions and sometimes resort to aggressive behavior to counter what they see as essentially a threat. Basically they are insecure. They are frequently secretive and rather tense people, for whom life is very serious. Whenever they do a good job they find it difficult to accept the credit. However, having lived with fear all their lives, they readily identify with the underdogs and courageously champion their causes.

SIXES frequently choose the church, the law or the armed forces as careers.

Further Comments

_____

_____

_____

_____

_____

_____

_____
_____
_____
_____
_____
_____
_____
_____
_____
_____
_____
_____
_____
_____
_____
_____

Conversion

To achieve integration SIXES need to take on the best aspects of the NINE. This will help them to:

• *Become calmer and more peaceful,* rather than fearful and full of doubt. It is vital that they believe that there is nothing that can destroy their deepest selves.

• *Trust others more and become less suspicious.* When they let others know they love them, they are loved in return. There is enough love to go around.

• *Take responsibility for their own actions,* instead of pretending to be obeying orders. They need to become more their own person and stop hiding behind the shield of authority.

• *Avoid overreacting.* In times of stress and anxiety they need to control their fear about the imagined outcome.

• *Be more direct in communicating.* This involves being open and clear about feelings, and not giving mixed signals.

SEVENS

IDENTITY CARD

NAME:	Optimist
IDENTITY:	I'm happy
CENTER:	Head
COMPULSION:	Optimism
PASSION:	Gluttony
OUTLET:	Planning
FEAR:	Pain
REJECTION:	Pain
DEFENSE:	Rationalization
FOCUS:	Fun and Plans
STANCE:	Smaller/Dependent
NEED:	Balance
HEALING:	God's Creative Helpers
VIRTUE:	Temperance

Childhood

As children SEVENS are cheerful, enthusiastic little extroverts—attractive, amusing, full of charm and fun, forever on the go. But this masks the fact that deep down they are frightened and afraid. In an attempt to diffuse their pain and divert their attention to other more pleasant things, they move out toward people. In later life they have very selective memories about their childhood, remembering only the good times, shutting out the bad. There may be many reasons for their feeling fearful—parents who don't ever want them to grow up; the loss of someone or something; parental unemployment or family poverty. Whatever it is, the child makes up for it with an over-active imagination and lifestyle which concentrates on the positive and superficial, allowing no time to come to terms with the negative and unpleasant realities of life.

Compulsion

SEVENS are gregarious, cheerful, optimistic and full of energy. But they will do anything they can to avoid pain in all its forms. Living is meant to be enjoyable, so they make sure they are always on the go and have a full program of activities lined up. This ensures that they keep out of the line of fire. They want to see, do and experience everything. Consequently they don't pursue things with the kind of single-mindedness often needed to rise to the top. Having a multitude of friends and activities means that the loss of one does not create an empty hole which cannot be filled. It has the added advantage that they will never be bored. They are excellent conversationalists, with a fund of stories.

The variety of interests and speed with which they move about burns up their energies, giving them an excuse for not dealing with deeper and more complex personal, social and spiritual issues. This means that they find commitment to causes or to people difficult to maintain. SEVENS are free spirits who hate to be tied down or to make priority choices. They are superficial rather than deep and can be narcissistic. They dislike confrontation and generally run away from it by involving themselves in more pleasant activities or even in addictive behavior.

They are frequently "con artists" who can charm the birds from the trees. They always have Plan B up their sleeve, with enough loopholes in both it and Plan A to allow them to escape if need be. They tend to be dreamers and future-orientated but want instant gratification, and can become very aggressive indeed when others try to set limits to their self-indulgence, forcing them to exercise restraint and self-control.

Given their talents they make good entertainers, musicians and writers (science fiction and children's stories).

Further Comments

_____

_____

_____

Conversion

To achieve integration SEVENS need to take on the best aspects of the FIVE. This will help them to:

• *Get to the heart of the matter,* rather than remain on the surface and risk being forever superficial.

• *Give rather than take.* They need to temper their thirst for instant gratification and "grab now" mentality and learn to contribute rather than consume.

• *Face the pain, not seek to avoid it.* They must stop trivializing serious issues. Making fun of problems will not make them go away or contribute towards a solution.

• *Control their impulsive nature.* It is important to know which enthusiasms to act on and which to control.

• *Learn the value of solitude and silence.* Their constant need for distractions and stimulation needs checking.

EIGHTS

```
IDENTITY CARD

NAME:            Leader
IDENTITY:        I'm powerful
CENTER:          Gut
COMPULSION:      Control
PASSION:         Lust
OUTLET:          Vengeance
FEAR:            Weakness
REJECTION:       Weakness
DEFENSE:         Denial
FOCUS:           Power and Justice
STANCE:          Bigger/Aggressive
NEED:            Tenderness
HEALING:         Compassion
VIRTUE:          Simplicity/Childlikeness
```

Childhood

Children who are EIGHTS quickly intuit that they can become the boss by denying their fear and vulnerability and using their power. They learn that if they assert themselves aggressively enough they can dictate the rules of the game and always get their way. Shouting, anger, vandalism and other such tactics allow them to dominate parents and others without any really painful comeback. Since we all imagine that other people are no different from ourselves, EIGHTS think that others also enjoy standing up for themselves. Consequently, they pay little attention to the feelings of others, refuse to say they're sorry and never ask for forgiveness. They learn to deny their feelings of guilt, and are quick to exploit any weakness they see. Always spoiling for a fight, they sometimes end up as delinquents.

Compulsion

EIGHTS are the most aggressive of all the types and love to

confront, intimidate and dominate others. They see life as a struggle to become "top dog" and in the process can ruthlessly put other people down, especially by attacking them at their weakest point. They say "no" more readily than "yes." They can be scathing in their criticisms and coarse in their use of language. They are self-assertive attention-getters and bulldoze their way through others if given half a chance. They despise weakness and only respect those who are ready to stand up for themselves.

However, they are also willing to take risks and stand up for the "underdog," particularly when they are the victims of injustice or oppression. At their best they see justice as an important value. If they are convinced that something is right they will be fiercely courageous in championing it. They work with zeal and intensity when they are involved in a project. They love a challenge and don't count the cost. They are very protective of their friends and of those in their care, but their relationships are generally based on possessiveness and submission.

Anger is their way of getting at the truth. They provoke people to find out what makes them tick. It is important to them that they be in control of people and events. They do not like surprises, especially in dealing with people. They like to get things out in the open and are highly confrontational. If they are dissatisfied with something, they will say so. They do not like pretense, deception or underhanded methods and constantly seek to expose and unmask these in others.

With their talents they may have become public prosecutors, chief executives, missionaries, or even dictators.

Further Comments

_____

_____

_____

_____

_____

_____

_____

_____

_____

_____

_____

_____

_____

_____

_____

_____

_____

_____

_____

_____

_____

Conversion

To achieve integration EIGHTS need to take on the best aspects of the TWO. This will help them to:

•*Acknowledge that others have rights too.* They must not be ignored, bullied, taken advantage of or dominated.

•*Own the tender side of their nature.* Growth happens when they accept their gentler feelings and reveal their wounds and weaknesses. This is a sign of real strength.

•*Accept that no one can be self-sufficient.* Dependence on others is part of being human, and acknowledging that means letting others take control and appreciating their help.

•*Learn to use their power for people,* rather than against them. This involves standing up for others, fighting their battles and inspiring them to stand on their own two feet.

•*Develop their magnanimity and generosity.* Self-interest is not the goal of life and money is more than a power tool.

NINES

IDENTITY CARD

NAME:	Mediator
IDENTITY:	I'm easy-going
CENTER:	Gut
COMPULSION:	Inaction
PASSION:	Laziness
OUTLET:	Indolence
FEAR:	Conflict
REJECTION:	Conflict
DEFENSE:	Narcotization
FOCUS:	Peace and Conflict
STANCE:	Adjust/Withdrawing
NEED:	Action
HEALING:	Love
VIRTUE:	Diligence

Childhood

Typically, nothing really matters to NINES, least of all themselves. This is because they seem to be continually overlooked by parents or other significant adults. They are not really listened to and cannot even get attention by becoming angry. Brothers or sisters may be preferred to them. They interpret all this as saying that they are not important enough to be loved and they cope with it by denying their own worth. Even at this early stage NINES compensate for an apparent lack of affection by turning to substitutes—excessive eating, reading and watching television. They are often placid, easy-going children, whose colorless appearance and voice indicate that they don't have much self-esteem. They learn not to bother, not to make an effort and not to show their anger.

Compulsion

NINES are very easy-going and prone to indecision and indolence. Yet they expend a great deal of energy trying to avoid conflict. They are the great "peacemakers." They want harmony, and are willing to resign themselves to difficult situations and play down problems rather than face the aggravation of dealing with them. They regularly buy time to get out of making decisions, and are even ready to make "molehills out of mountains" in order to maintain the peace.

Since nothing matters all that much and nobody is more important than anyone else, NINES are generally unshockable. They are very tolerant and accepting of people, no matter how awkward or difficult. They are non-judgmental and non-threatening, always willing to balance one view with another. They are unassuming and receptive and are, therefore, very comfortable and calming to be with. However, although they like you, they give the impression that they would like someone else just as well. They daydream a lot.

They are sometimes surprisingly busy people, but they concern themselves with doing non-essential things since they find it hard to distinguish between these and what is really important. They find it difficult to decide on priorities or to keep focused. Since they try not to get excited about things, time just passes them by. Being late doesn't bother them and they are often forgetful. They procrastinate a lot. They love being rooted in their own space.

They don't trust themselves. Though they have undoubted talents, they are uneasy with compliments. They prefer to remain out of the limelight in case people begin to expect too much from them. They need to remain in control and for that reason don't like surprises. They can "dig in" and become quite stubborn, but generally keep their anger in check.

The NINES make excellent negotiators, mediators, counsellors and facilitators.

Further Comments

_____

_____

_____

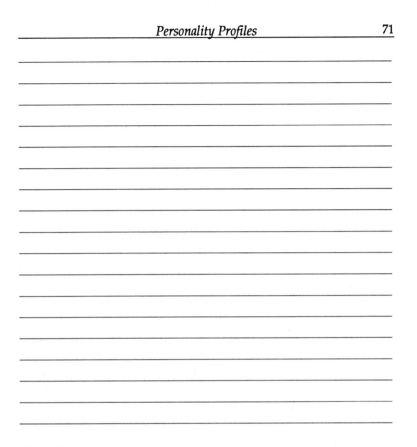

Conversion

To achieve integration NINES need to take on the best aspects of the THREE. This will help them to:

•*Acknowledge their own self-worth.* This is their greatest need. They cannot love and appreciate others if they do not love and appreciate themselves.

•*Take control of their lives.* They need to rouse themselves out of their complacency and become involved in life.

•*Face the tensions and conflicts,* and avoid trying to make things peaceful and tranquil at any price.

•*Deal with negative feelings,* and try not to paper over the cracks. They need to own their aggression and stubbornness.

•*Confront all forms of narcotization and escapism.* Life is full of problems and tranquilizers are no solution.

5

HEALING OUR BROKENNESS

Broken people are beautiful. There is something about vulnerability, suffering and pain that the human heart responds to instinctively. We become sympathetic, tender, warm and protective towards those whose wounds show through their skin. It doesn't matter whether these wounds are physical, psychological or spiritual. Brokenness in all its forms cries out to be healed. Our wounds speak louder than our words ever could.

The cry of the broken-hearted reaches out and doesn't stop until it finds God, who holds all things in being. The Christian message is that, in Jesus, God has sent his own Son to become truly human, to share our brokenness. In doing so he revealed to us that we are all broken people, whether we know it or not.

There are so many ways in which we are broken. When we are neglected and left alone, something inside us is torn. When we are physically, emotionally or sexually abused, something inside us snaps. When we feel unwanted or betrayed, our heart is wounded. When we experience empty promises and religious doubts, our spirits falter. When we are burdened with shame and tortured with guilt, the pain is always there. When we taste depression and are filled with fear, we find ourselves being ripped asunder. When we no longer find sense or meaning in our lives, we reach the depths of despair.

The central core of the gospel story is that, no matter how broken we are, we are all beautiful and we are all loved. Regardless of what scars we carry, we are loved with an incredible intensity by God. This love is shown in the way Jesus healed the sick, the blind, the deaf, the lame, the lepers, the bereaved, the possessed—the entire company of walking wounded whose hurt called forth such a tender response. This love is expressed in its darkest form in a bruised, battered body nailed to a wooden cross. To be broken is not something irreparable. In the death and resurrection of Christ our wounds have been bound up and healed.

One of the most important things that the Enneagram tells us is that we are all different, that we all have characteristic and appropriate ways of doing things which are fundamentally related to our particular outlook, to the driving force of our lives. Each one of us sees reality from a different perspective. We don't stand in each other's shoes, but make our own distinctive footprints on the path of life.

It follows, therefore, that we do not all go to God in the same way, that there is no one path to holiness and, consequently, no one "right" way to pray. In terms of the Enneagram our approach to God will be at one with the center of our basic energy, whether that be our gut, our heart, or our head. We pray and go to God as we are, not as we are not.

The Face of God
The Bible speaks of humanity as being created in the image and likeness of God (cf. Genesis 1:27). The traditional presentation of the Enneagram takes this for granted but goes on to point out that, just as humanity is made up of nine essentially different personality types, so the divine image in humanity is manifested in nine different ways.

Each one of us has been created with certain gifts and qualities which reflect one aspect of the "Face of God" to the world, gifting others with the reminder of God's presence in our own characteristic fashion. This is our unique privilege and our central task in life. "Where the Spirit of the Lord is, there is freedom. And we, with our unveiled faces reflecting like mirrors the brightness of the Lord, all grow brighter and brighter as we are turned into the image that we reflect; this is the work of the Lord who is Spirit." (2 Corinthians 3:17-18)

Part of our problem is that, as we go through life, the struggle between good and evil leads to a division within us and we manage to distort this image and twist this gift. Instead of reflecting the divine image we begin to polish up and reflect our own. We become egocentric and selfish and hide behind a mask of our own making. We try to be God in our own lives, relying on our own efforts to achieve holiness, holding on to life with both hands in case by letting go we would somehow cease to be. In doing so we effectively turn what should be our best gift into our most troublesome sin. The way in which we transform our God-given giftedness into our own manufactured image is in reality our capital sin—the root way in which we put our own face, not God's before the world.

If we do not open our inner door and let God in, we shut ourselves off from the truth. The result is that we become increasingly narrow-minded and prepared to live a lie. When we keep our door closed we are no longer free, because in the long run it is only the truth that makes us free (cf. John 8:32).

The Enneagram helps us face the truth about ourselves. In doing so it both shames us and liberates us. It is embarrassing to have our false selves unmasked and revealed for what they are. But, at the same time, having nothing to hide behind frees us and allows us to grow towards wholeness.

On our way to God, to wholeness and holiness, we don't always manage to stay on the right road. We get side-tracked by siren voices and wander up a variety of cul-de-sacs; we may even take a totally different route so that when, eventually, we look at the signposts to see where we're headed, we find that they point in the wrong direction altogether.

But that's life; that's part of our brokenness. Although we are created fundamentally good, none of us goes through life undamaged. In addition to our inherited genetic programming and the conditioning of our family, educational and social environment, we are also caught up in the original sinfulness of our human condition. This regularly prevents us from reaching our spiritual goal, as the Greek word for sin, *hamartia* ("missing the mark") highlights. So, we all need healing and redemption.

God's Initiative, Our Response

Jesus is the one who shows us what God is like and what human beings can be like when they live in union with God. As Christians we believe that Jesus Christ is our redeemer, and that redemption is a gift given to us in Christ. We cannot merit it by what we do; it is not something we achieve by our own efforts. But God has also given us the freedom to choose and does not force that choice. This implies that we *can* do something to prepare ourselves for God's grace, and to open ourselves to the promptings of the Spirit. It is also the reason why many of the saints have counselled us to pray as if everything depended on God and to act as if everything depended on ourselves.

The Enneagram is a great help to those of us who want to open ourselves to the healing power of God. It allows us to see our hidden sinfulness with a clarity which we might never experience in any other way. It shows us our predominant fault and how it is that we remain fixed in our ego when what we want more than anything else is to break out of its grasp. As Paul put it so poignantly: "I cannot understand my own behavior. I fail to carry out the things I want to do, and I find myself doing the very things I hate." (Romans 7:15)

We all look at life from an egocentric perspective. We are stuck in our narrow way of looking at things, frequently supposing that everybody else looks at things the same way and, worse again, that this is the only perspective possible. We have made ourselves the measure of everything. We have locked ourselves into seeing and hearing only what our built-in biases allow us to see and hear. We have shaped reality to fit our own prejudiced view of it. As if that were not bad enough, we try to shape God in the same way.

What the Enneagram does is reveal to us at depth that what we are seeing is distorted by our own typical outlook and that there are eight other basic and very different ways of viewing reality. When we stick to our own grasp of the truth we immediately limit it. We are caught in a vicious circle which, far from leading us to God, simply leads us back to our own narrow window on the world.

Using the Enneagram helps us focus on this shadow side. In its traditional presentation it opens us up to the spiritual dimension within us, to our need for conversion and to our inability to turn our lives around by our own unaided efforts. It is, therefore, a very helpful tool for spiritual discernment. It reveals the lies which masquerade as the truth. It brings out into the light the selfish energies which fuel our activity. It helps us distinguish between what is authentic and what is not. It identifies the traps into which we regularly fall and the protective barriers we put up to avoid being touched, "got at" or hurt. It allows us to discern whether our personal house is built on rock or on sand.

The fundamental assumption of our consumer society is that we are what we have. But if we are what we have, what are we when what we have is taken away? An essential part of the gospel message is that what counts is not what we have but who we are. The Enneagram takes away our crutches and gives us the freedom to walk our own gifted path.

Our Brokenness
Spirituality is the way we respond to the presence of God in our lives. St. Irenaeus of Lyons had a beautifully perceptive insight into the significance of the Incarnation. He said: "What is not accepted is not redeemed." Because we wholeheartedly agree with this, we have chosen to follow a very simple procedure in the rest of this section.

The first step is to identify our core sin, to *name it* in all its stark reality. Having done so, we then *claim it* as our own, acknowledging its specific dominance in our lives. Finally, we learn to *tame it*, especially by means of the help obtained through scriptural meditation and prayer. The prayers which open each section are fundamentally positive. They affirm and express gratitude for our essential giftedness and ask for healing in our brokenness. The concluding practical suggestions for each personality type indicate what might be of particular help to us in opening ourselves to God.

Our core sins really are killers because frequently we don't even know or acknowledge that they are ours. We admit to many faults but *not* to our central, most deadly one. "That's not me at all," we say. But it is. The problem is that very often we don't see what others see, because we are so successful at keeping it hidden from ourselves. We have many ways of escaping our inner pain. We are endlessly creative at devising defense mechanisms to protect us from our central compulsion.

Most of us are put off by books on spirituality with grandiose titles. But we can all readily identify with the notion of brokenness because we have all been wounded by life, we all have our inner place of pain. We can relate with broken people because we know that vulnerability is part of the fallen human condition, that we are not angels but embodied spirits. This is what it means to take our humanity seriously.

On a personal note, we ourselves have both seen children and adults who have been wounded and hurt by others, sometimes even by those who were supposed to have been their healers. At home and abroad, at work and in counselling situations, looking into our hearts and sharing our own stories, we have come to realize the ache within us all. In our own lives, too, both of us have experienced physical, emotional, psychological and spiritual brokenness. We consider this to be a blessing, because it has made us realize the need we have for the healing power of God's love.

Openness to Change
The Enneagram is only a tool. Of itself it has no power to save. For us, as Christians, Christ is the one who saves. But one of the great strengths of the Enneagram is that it allows us to see clearly the hidden source of our individual brokenness and increases our compassion for the pain this brings. It is a powerful tool for showing us the shadow side of our personality— our compulsions, our addictions, our dysfunctional patterns of behavior and, above all, our hidden sin.

In the previous chapter we concentrated on profiling the nine basic compulsive energies which drive us. Now we concentrate on how we can grow in and through our brokenness.

This will take time and is not going to be easy. In the spiritual life, too, there is no such thing as a free lunch. We generally get what we pay for. But it is our belief that we will also get what we pray for.

On our spiritual journey towards conversion we can be as imaginative and inventive as we like. What's important is that we begin. It's amazing how differently we think about things when we pray about them. Prayer helps us see things from God's perspective. In the process we develop a whole new way of looking at the world. This, in turn, gradually leads to a radical change of heart. Our prayer is that we will all experience the healing power of God's love.

ONES

DAILY PRAYER

Lord God, I thank you for giving me
a keen sense of what is right
and a diligent desire to do good.
In my attempts to live up to my ideals,
help me to be patient and forgiving.
Teach me to be tolerant of mistakes
rather than always finding fault with things.
Show me how to accept what is good enough
and, above all, how to lighten up,
enjoy life and gently relax in your love. Amen.

Name It

My Name:	The Perfectionist
My Vice:	Anger
My God:	The All-Perfect, Just Judge
My Masks:	Resentment, Anxiety, Rigidity, Jealousy
My Need:	Patience
My Virtue:	Serenity

Claim It

Deep down I'm very angry. That's my brokenness. I don't normally admit this. I generally cover it up so that nobody knows. But the tenseness of my body, in particular my face, often betrays me. I have a very strong sense of right and wrong and an inner voice criticizes me when I fail. I don't want to be seen as a hypocrite. I do so want to measure up to what God expects of me. The trouble is that I also want to achieve the impossibly high standards I frequently set for myself. And because I don't, I am fundamentally angry—at God for not creating me perfect in the first place, at others for contributing to the mess the world is in, and at myself for not arriving more rapidly at what I consider to be spiritual wholeness. Time just runs away from me and I think I'll never make it.

I always want to live from strength, not weakness. So a spirituality of self-control rather than of brokenness is much more my style. I dislike the cold shell I have constructed because it makes it difficult for others to get to know me, and gives the impression that I am dismissive of people. In reality, though, it is only a way of protecting myself from getting hurt and from letting others see that I bleed too.

Other people seem to have a much easier life and I resent that. Because I see so clearly the faults in everything and everyone, I have become judgmental, critical and negative. Only grudgingly and with deliberate effort am I a source of affirmation and praise. I often think that when I share what little goodness I have, I somehow diminish my own store of it.

Lord God, there are times when I look at myself and see only a sinner and you as a Just Judge who will make me pay for all my imperfections. I know that both of these are inadequate and that in reality you are wonderfully compassionate and I am fundamentally good. I just need to be patient, to do what I can and then to wait for the growth which comes through your healing touch.

Tame It

Allowing God to work in us, to heal our anger and ease our pain is a life-long process. We mustn't be impatient or want everything "now." A spirituality which is strongly influenced by social justice issues is attractive to our type, given our interest in putting things right and transforming the mess.

However, the quiet, gentle approach is often what we need most. This is all the more important since we experience the world as being bigger than we are. It follows that we feel we have to work harder to control our environment and set things right. When we let God be God and not take on ourselves the burden of single-handedly trying to improve on creation, we will save ourselves a lot of needless anxiety.

The following suggestions for reflection and prayer, though not exhaustive, may help.

■ *Matthew 10:1-16 (The workers in the vineyard)*
This parable makes us face up to the reality that life is not about fairness, but about gift. We are invited to become co-workers in building the Kingdom. But God's generosity is always unconditional and does not depend on our effort. Still less does it depend on keeping lists of rules and regulations, like the Pharisees to whom it was originally addressed.

■ *Luke 15:11-32 (The parable of the prodigal son)*
Reflecting on the role of the elder, dutiful son in this parable brings us face to face with our own moralistic self-righteousness. Like him, our spiritual hit-list may well include members of our own family. While we make every effort to contain our anger, it generally comes out in the form of resentment. The model Jesus offers us is that of the compassionate father.

■ *Luke 6:41-42 (On not being so judgmental)*
Our over-ready ability to see the faults in others often blinds us to similar faults in ourselves. Sometimes we miss the woods for the trees. Tolerance of mistakes and a willingness to learn are gospel values worth cultivating.

■ *Mark 12:31 (Self-love is a condition for loving others)*
In general we are far too hard on ourselves. We never let up. Jesus teaches us that we are fundamentally good rather than flawed. We cannot love others unless we first love ourselves.

■ *Matthew 13:24-30 (Waiting for growth)*
We find it difficult to tolerate imperfection and ambiguity, so we are frequently seduced by the urgency of our desire for clean-cut immediate solutions. But real life is messy. We need to trust God and be patient with ourselves and others.

Further Comments

_____

_____

_____

_____

_____

_____

_____

_____

_____

_____

_____

_____

_____

_____

_____

_____

_____

_____

_____

_____

_____

PRACTICAL SUGGESTION

◇◇◇ *We are high-energy people who are relentless in our pursuit of justice, right and moral perfection. What we need is to experience the peace and tranquility of being quiet in God's presence. It helps to find a comfortable posture and relax tense muscles. An icon or other symbol may prove useful to get us started. There is no need for us to worry about putting words to our prayer. Since time is so important to us, having a set time for prayer each day helps. What we are trying to foster is receptivity and the generosity of "letting go." This will make it easier to forget our cares, concerns and current involvements and assist in calming our restless analytical minds.*

TWOS

DAILY PRAYER

Lord God, I thank you for giving me
the gift of a generous heart.
Help me to understand that
your love for me does not depend
on what I do for other people.
Show me how to minister to
the needs of others
without losing sight of my own.
Allow me to feel in my own wounds
the healing power of your love. Amen.

Name It

My Name:	The Helper
My Vice:	Pride
My God:	The Eternal Caregiver
My Masks:	Flattery, Privilege, Ambition, Seduction
My Need:	Acceptance of real worth
My Virtue:	Humility

Claim It

Deep down I'm proud. That's my brokenness. I feel I'm better than others because I'm generally more caring. I see the needs of others even before they do themselves and do everything I can to help them, sometimes without even being asked. I constantly put myself out to be of service, but I also expect people to recognize and appreciate what I do for them.

However, when I really think about it, I know that my helpfulness is both a source of recognition and a way of seeing myself as being of value. I know that what appears to others as selfless and generous is not entirely so. There are often strings attached. I exercise pressure indirectly and by stealth. I don't blatantly seek to manipulate, but I know that what I do is manipulative nonetheless. Being helpful is my way of getting attention, of asking for love without putting it into words. It feels good to have people who depend on me. Their need gives me a sense of being important, useful and worthwhile. It helps define who I am.

Lord God, I know this means I don't have a good self-image, and that I don't appreciate the gift you have given me. You love me unconditionally. I don't have to keep proving myself, to you or to anyone else. I don't have to try so hard to please all the time. Love cannot be earned or paid for. It is always a gift. Help me to realize that the needs I perceive in others are often a reflection of those within myself. Give me the humility to accept that I, too, am in need of help.

Tame It

Our constant concern for others frequently masks the lack of attention we pay to our own physical, emotional, psychological and spiritual needs. We help others and neglect ourselves. But if we're always giving, always active, is there anything for ourselves when at some point we stop the treadmill? Who fills the emptiness of our personal storehouse?

We need to learn the spiritual truth that "charity begins at home," that without a realistic acceptance of our own woundedness, we cannot even begin to understand the pain of others let alone help them alleviate it. We have to learn to make the journey inward. In doing so, since we have lived so long with our need to be needed, we shouldn't be surprised to find ourselves acting out of it, even when we've made significant efforts to counter its grip. We need the humility to accept our brokenness and the patience to allow God's love to heal our wounds.

The following suggestions for reflection and prayer, though not exhaustive, may help.

■ *Luke 10:38-42 (Martha and Mary)*
In God's presence everything is placed in its proper perspective. Mary is praised because she allows the Lord to min-

ister to her needs before she ministers to those of others. God has no need of the martyr complex. Martha manipulatively tries to get Jesus on her side and urges him to proclaim the importance of service. Instead, she learns that this is but one value among others. Hospitality, duty and task-sharing are undoubtedly important, but only one thing is essential.

■ *Mark 12:31 (Love others as you love yourself)*
It is important to put first things first. Charity begins at home for the good reason that if we are not loving towards ourselves we cannot possibly be loving towards others. Care, compassion and respect for the self are essential prerequisites for extending them to others.

■ *Mark 10:35-44 (A lesson in humility)*
James and John let their pride run away with them. They were prepared to suffer anything provided they got the highest places in the Kingdom. But Jesus reminds us all that genuine service is not a power-play. When we look for preferment we are effectively attached to a false self-image, one which is fundamentally empty and in need of shoring up.

■ *Mark 14:32-42 (Facing our inner fears)*
Jesus was no stranger to feelings. In Gethsemane he experienced inner distress and great fear. He shared these feelings with his friends and wasn't ashamed to ask for their help. Indeed, his loneliness was compounded by their weakness.

■ *Luke 4:42-44 (The right to say "no")*
We need to give proper time to our own spiritual needs and not allow our compulsive generosity to rule our lives. Saying "no" to others should not make us feel guilty. They have no right to the last drop.

Further Comments

_____

_____

_____

_____

PRACTICAL SUGGESTION

◇◇◇ *Since we undervalue our own needs it is important to find a place (in a family, community or among friends) where we, too, are looked after. But we also need to make a space in our day for ourselves alone. During this time it is vital to concentrate on being rather than doing. First we need to relax. Aromatherapy may help, or listening to some soothing meditative music. However, this is but a preparation for our doing some serious inner work. We have to face our own wounds, our own neediness—the personal concerns we regularly set aside for the sake of ministering to others. Having named one, we can pray about it and offer it to God for healing.*

THREES

DAILY PRAYER

Lord God, I thank you for creating me
in your image and for blessing me
with the drive and energy to succeed.
Help me to realize that
achievement isn't everything,
and that failure can often provide
more truth than success.
Show me how to get beneath
the surface images I love to create
to the even more beautiful center within. Amen.

Name It

My Name:	The Achiever
My Vice:	Deceit
My God:	The Successful Creator
My Masks:	Vanity, Security, Prestige, Ideal Image
My Need:	Examine the Image
My Virtue:	Truth

Claim It

Deep down I'm deceitful. That's my brokenness. I cover it up so that it's even hidden from myself. I'm radically out of touch with my innermost depths of feeling and love. I keep myself constantly busy so as not to have to face my real self. I am skilled at covering up, at showing a different face for every possible occasion. Pretense comes naturally to me, as I strive to be a winner in everything I do.

I court success, security and prestige because I'm afraid of failure. I don't stop long enough to face the truth behind the masks of my own making. I know I need to learn the success of apparent failure and the failure of what sometimes looks like success. I need to absorb the lesson of the cross, the glory of failure, the economy of grace.

I'm ever restless, always on the move, never still. I prefer to be a moving target rather than a sitting duck. I give the impression that I have made it, that everything comes so easily to me. But in reality, I'm living a lie.

Lord God, there are times when I see myself as a superficial shell, and you as the Successful Creator with whom I long to compete. I know that neither of these is the whole truth. You created me in your image, yet I have spent much of my life trying to embellish it to my own liking, hiding your beautiful handiwork under a constant series of masks.

I know you love me in spite of my duplicity and image-making. You are interested in the reality, not in the substitute image. You see the human vulnerable face behind my high-profile. self-sufficient mask. Help me to get in touch with my need for others, with the tender side of my heart and with the truth beyond the soft option and the hard sell.

Show me that what I achieve in worldly terms is as nothing to the generosity of your passionate love. My life is lived at a frenetic pace, but you see the still center where my heart aches and I crave for love. Slow me down, Lord, so that I can with calm heart know the real secret of creative love.

Tame It

Risking the self-revelation and self-giving of love takes time. Our defenses have been built up over many years. Deceit is not healed in a day. The failures we experience as we grow in a spirituality of radical truthfulness should be an encouragement to us that we are moving in the direction of wholeness. For us the movement is from the external to the internal. What we *do* is undoubtedly important, but what we *are* is vital. Like all other personality types we have to keep a proper balance between *being* and *doing*.

The following suggestions for reflection and prayer, though not exhaustive, may help.

■ *John 8:32 (The truth will set us free)*
Our constant movement may seduce us into thinking that we are genuinely free spirits. However, true freedom consists not in running away, but in standing one's ground. It is not pretense but honesty. Truth, not the sophisticated veneer of self-deception, is what will make us free.

■ *Luke 9:46-48 (Who is the greatest in the Kingdom?)*
Position, prestige and privilege cut no ice with Jesus. Our emphasis on the significant roles we play does not impress him. What does get through is a childlike heart—the ability to live life without duplicity.

■ *Luke 18:9-14 (The Pharisee and the publican)*
Never mind the quality, feel the width! We are well able to show off, to boast about our achievements, to imagine that once we have successfully managed our image we have somehow made it. But God is not impressed by the vanity of self-advertisement. If we pray like that we will end up like the Pharisee—talking to ourselves.

■ *John 6:63-71 (The loyalty of the true follower)*
When we truly believe, we must be prepared to be faithful. We have difficulty with that. We are inclined to abandon projects in mid-stream if there is a danger that their failure will tarnish our image. We need reminding that if we don't stand for something, we are in danger of falling for anything.

■ *John 15:13-17 (Love is the key)*
God judges us on the quality of our love, not on who we know or what our qualifications are. We need friendship in our lives. We need to see God as a loving friend, who knows our weakness and chooses us regardless. We are called to go beyond the exterior in our dealings with others, so that our love is both true and sincere.

Further Comments

_____

_____

_____

_____

_____

_____

_____

_____

_____

_____

_____

_____

_____

_____

_____

_____

_____

_____

_____

_____

_____

PRACTICAL SUGGESTION

◊◊◊ *Since we tend to be out of touch with our emotions it is important to tap this source of energy in prayer. Generally we find that our emotions slow us down and don't allow us to be as productive and efficient as we want to be. But prayer is more about presence than productivity, about wasting time creatively rather than having something to show for it. Far from being boring, such time-wasting can prove to be deeply energizing. Using music and posture to introduce us to the stillness of our center can be very helpful. Also, since movement is one of our strengths, why not harness it in our prayer? Dance, drama o simple repetitive movement may be useful here.*

FOURS

DAILY PRAYER

Lord God, I thank you for giving me
a keen eye for beauty and
a special sensitivity to the human heart.
Show me how even the most ordinary
and everyday realities are filled
with the wonder of your presence.
Help me to live in the present moment
and to appreciate that my
tears and laughter, joy and pain
are part of your loving plan for the world. Amen.

Name It

My Name:	The Artist
My Vice:	Envy
My God:	Sensitive Creator of Beauty
My Masks:	Melancholy, Resistance, Shame, Competition
My Need:	Sense of present reality
My Virtue:	Equanimity (Harmony)

Claim It

Deep down I'm envious. That's my brokenness. I'm usually too ashamed or too caught up in my own feelings to admit this. I'm so afraid of the pain of rejection. I long to be special, to be different, somehow to rise above the ordinary and the mundane. I am especially sensitive to beauty in all its forms. I love anything which is simple, natural, authentic. My standards are so high that the more I try to reach them, the more artificial I become. I can't help comparing myself with people who have more talent, taste, sophistication and class than I have and longing to be somehow superior.

I envy them the ease with which they seem to live their

lives. It's easier for me to live in memories, dreams and the world of the arts than in the everyday world, where the mess is part of the reality. I have real problems with intimacy and distance. What I have, I don't value; what I long for, I treasure. I'm regularly disappointed by life and this makes me sad. Why is it that others seem to have it all? Even in my relationships I'm jealous of others being somehow more interesting or attractive than I am. I'm ashamed of my body, my inner turmoil disgusts me and I regularly run myself down. Is it any wonder that I have a poor self-image?

Lord God, all of this causes me intense inner suffering. I go through a roller-coaster of feelings, from ecstatic joy to inexpressible sadness. People think this is just moodiness. If only they knew how deep it goes, they'd see what a dreadful burden it is.

Life is such a struggle for me, Lord, yet I'm tragically unwilling to accept help. Please help me. Help me to appreciate the special sensitivity and intuition you have given me—the ability to understand at depth the emotional life of others. Show me how to be realistic enough not to imagine this world as the safe haven of my dreams, but as holding in balance tears and laughter, pain and joy, ugliness and beauty, violence and peace. Help me not to be so elitist, so snobbish, but to value the normal, the ordinary and the everyday.

Tame It
For us the movement is from the romanticized memories of the past and the hoped-for visions of the future to the humdrum reality of the present. We need to learn to be at ease and content with the way things are, understanding that "God is in the pots and pans" (Teresa of Avila), that we meet God in the ordinary, the everyday, the mundane, the pedestrian, the hackneyed. Rather than bemoan people's misunderstanding of who we are, we should try to use our talents for drama, ritual, art, music, poetry and symbol to give a powerful voice to those who cannot speak as eloquently or protest as imaginatively as we can. But we must not be surprised if it takes time for us to readjust our priorities in this way.

The following suggestions for reflection and prayer, though not exhaustive, may help.

■ *Matthew 6:25-34 (Everything is in God's hands)*
Nothing is ordinary in God's sight. Even the birds of the air and the grass in the fields take on a numinous significance, an eternal aspect which reflects the tender care of the Creator. We are no less special or cared for than they. The ordinary is energized when seen in this light, and distinctions between sacred and secular disappear.

■ *Matthew 18:23-35 (The unforgiving steward)*
Jesus tells us that when we are consumed with our own self-interest we lose our sense of proportion, our compassion and our sensitivity to others.

■ *Mark 10:13-16 (Like little children)*
Children are still open to the wonder of life. They have not lost their delight in the everyday. Familiarity has not yet led them to contempt. They see the beauty of things with innocent eyes and listen to their truth with a welcoming heart.

■ *John 19:1-11 (Being crowned with thorns)*
Jesus experienced abandonment and rejection in dramatic fashion towards the end of his life. But, however humiliated, he relied on God's help and placed himself in God's care.

■ *John 2:1-12 (The wedding at Cana)*
Everyday elements (water and wine) combined with a discerning heart can transform impending disasters into celebrations of joy. Like Jesus and Mary we can bring happiness to others by our sensitivity to their needs.

Further Comments

_____

_____

_____

_____

_____

_____

_____

_____

_____

_____

_____

_____

_____

_____

_____

_____

_____

_____

_____

PRACTICAL SUGGESTION

◇◇◇ *Our tendency is to live on the inside and over-emphasize our feelings. But, if we are to grow spiritually, it is vital that we learn to get our feelings in perspective, and get some balance into the relationship between our inner life and the messy reality around us. Yoga, massage, or aromatherapy may help us relax and become less intense. Journaling (keeping a record of what's happening in our lives) may help us distance ourselves from our feelings, and is a useful safety-valve for externalizing our inner concerns. Since relationships are very important to us, shared prayer and liturgy, and getting involved in social justice issues, can be especially meaningful and life-giving.*

FIVES

DAILY PRAYER

Lord God, I thank you for giving me
an enquiring mind and the gift of discernment.
Help me to reach out more to people,
and to trust the wisdom
that comes from the heart.
Give me the generosity
to share my insights with those I meet,
and the courage to involve myself
in their daily cares and concerns. Amen.

Name It

My Name:	The Observer
My Vice:	Avarice/Greed
My God:	The Ultimate Source of Meaning
My Masks:	Stinginess, Withdrawal, Guru, Confidence
My Need:	To get involved
My Virtue:	Detachment

Claim It

Deep down I'm greedy and avaricious, not so much for material things as for the knowledge that will give my life meaning. That's my brokenness. I find it hard to admit this, even to myself, and I have the skills to cover it up so that nobody knows. But the truth is that I'm so afraid of feeling empty inside that I continually long for fulfillment. I dread the idea of meaninglessness and my continual quest for knowledge is simply my way of dealing with this.

Sometimes I experience such great loneliness that the only way I can feel safe is to shut myself away, most frequently by living inside my head. I appear confident and self-assured on the surface, but deep down I experience a great deal of insecurity. I attempt to fill the void by my passion for collecting and hoarding. I don't like intrusions and am very protective of my own space.

I generally try to remain calm and keep my emotions under control. When I'm angry, upset, fearful or emotional, I try not to show it. But I do feel things deeply. It's just that I tend to analyze my feelings rather than immediately experience them. I find it hard to express my emotions or put them into words. It's much easier for me to show warmth towards friends who are absent rather than those who are present.

Lord God, you know me better than I do myself. You know how difficult it is for me to trust other people, to let go of my "fortress mentality," to avoid being cynical. I consider myself superior to others because I think I'm perceptive enough to see through their superficiality and sham. But the loss is mine, not theirs. I've lost the common touch because of my tendency to over-analyze everything.

Lord, I know I'm not the "giving" sort. I certainly find it very painful to get involved. I both long for and somehow feel threatened by intimacy. I don't look for attention and don't allow others the opportunity for making demands on me. I limit my contacts with people and compartmentalize my life precisely in order to avoid involvement. I prefer to retreat or intellectualize rather than get "stuck in."

Tame It

Our spiritual journey is from the internal to the external. It involves taking the incarnation seriously. It means accepting that knowledge comes through the heart and the senses as well as through the head. The fact is that God became flesh, not newsprint, and there's no escaping the implications of that. Unfortunately, there is a painful split within us between theory and practice, between contemplation and action. We must be bold enough to risk involvement, and inventive enough to give practical expression to our insights and reflections. Then we will not give in to disengagement and others will be able to share in the wisdom we have to offer.

The following suggestions for reflection and prayer, though not exhaustive, may help.

■ *John 9:39-41 (Those with sight can be blind to the truth)*
There is a difference between knowledge and wisdom, between sight and insight. What we think we know can blind us to other possibilities and prevent us from learning from the poor and needy who stand in front of our eyes.

■ *Luke 10:29-37 (The Good Samaritan)*
It is very easy to theorize and generalize about what needs to be done to provide a solution to people's problems. Noninvolvement is a form of opting out, of passing by "on the other side." Jesus demands that we give flesh to our beliefs and discover the truths that only touching the wounds can bring.

■ *Luke 6:38 (We receive in the measure that we give)*
Our unwillingness to risk sharing what we have with a generous heart frequently prevents us from receiving more ourselves. If we hoard what we have and are stingy with our gifts, we are unlikely to be open enough to receive the unexpected.

■ *John 11:32-44 (Jesus is moved to tears)*
We don't really trust our feelings. We find it hard to express emotion, to show how deeply we care for others. This gospel story shows how Jesus expresses his love unashamedly and does something constructive about it.

■ *Luke 11:9-13 (Ask and you will receive)*
It is difficult for us to ask for help to meet our needs or fill the empty place within our hearts. We much prefer to go it alone and make do. But God is the generous giver, whose compassionate presence brings love and meaning into our lives.

Further Comments

_____

_____

_____

_____

_____

_____

_____

_____

_____

_____

_____

_____

_____

_____

_____

PRACTICAL SUGGESTION

◇◇◇ *Since we tend to over-emphasize the mind and are open to a wide variety of prayer options, it is important for us to anchor our thoughts and get in touch with our heart. We can often best do this by concentrating on some symbol—a lighted candle, a cake of bread, a mantra, etc.—which will help us center our thoughts and not allow them to jump about in a free-fall meditation. Our body is very important in prayer, so posture, breathing, clothing, warmth, and so on are particularly relevant. All of these can keep us open to the promptings of the real world when we place ourselves in God's presence. In this way there will always be an active element in our contemplation.*

SIXES

DAILY PRAYER

Lord God, I thank you for giving me
a great respect for the law and
the gift of loyalty to friends.
Help me to understand more deeply
how much you really love me.
Safe in the knowledge of this love
and relying on your tender care,
may I have the courage to
overcome my fears and become
more trusting of myself and others. Amen.

Name It

My Name:	The Supporter
My Vice:	Fear/Anxiety
My God:	Ultimate Security
My Masks:	Doubt, Warmth, Obedience, Hard/Soft
My Need:	Faith
My Virtue:	Courage

Claim It

Deep down I'm full of fear. That's my brokenness. I'm not willing to admit it, but it comes out in my doubts and in my deeply anxious approach to life. I am very mistrustful—of myself and others. I seem to be continually watchful and afraid. My self-doubt and lack of self-confidence make me much too dependent on others, particularly on those in a position of authority. Relying on tradition, the law and the institutions of society gives me a great sense of security and helps allay my fear of making a mistake.

I find it difficult to trust my own abilities and instincts. Yet, at the same time, I do not completely trust others. I can spot danger a mile off and am quick to look for cover. I prefer to see things in straightforward terms, in black and white rather than shades of grey. I like to be sure of my position and not contradict myself. To do so, I pay attention to detail. The trouble is that I then find it hard to make up my mind. I either hesitate and allow myself to be led by others, or I over-compensate, become obstinate, defiant and take risks.

Even though I work well in a group, the model I work out of is hierarchical. There is a sense in which my loyalty to the group is just an expression of my basic insecurity—a way of finding strength in numbers. I don't really have the courage of my own convictions. Indeed, my sense of duty is often a cover for my anxiety about making decisions for myself. What it amounts to is a fear of freedom, a fundamental unwillingness to say "yes" or "no" on my own.

Lord God, what I need is faith in you and in my own goodness. I find it difficult to accept undiluted praise because I don't really believe in my own value and worth. But you have given me a wonderful variety of talents and gifts, and called me into your close circle of friends.

Help me to realize, Lord, that you do not expect impossible standards from me. Give me the faith to believe that you love me for who I am. Give me the courage to take responsibility for my day-to-day choices. Help me to give myself permission to own my feelings and to open myself up to you and others in a relationship of mutual trust and intimacy.

Tame It
Our spiritual journey is from the inside out, from self-protective assessment to courageous commitment. We have to venture forth and risk the possibility of getting shot down. We cannot keep backing out of life, refusing to make decisions or get involved for fear of what might go wrong. We have a "stop-go" mentality, an "on-off" approach. If we wait until we have certitude we will never act at all. True discipleship involves costly action. Trust in God means facing our fear of the unfamiliar, the unknown and the unexpected.

The following suggestions for reflection and prayer, though not exhaustive, may help.

■ *Matthew 25:14-30 (Parable of the talents)*
This parable is essentially about seizing the opportunity when it is presented, rather than being so cautious that we allow ourselves to be paralyzed by fear.

■ *John 20:24-29 (Doubt no more, but believe)*
We like certainties and find it difficult to cope with doubt, ambiguity or loose ends. We are afraid to risk committing ourselves without supporting evidence. Our search for verification can even lead us to withdraw from others and in so doing miss the unexpected truth. But God is patient with us and gently leads us to inner conviction and faith.

■ *Mark 2:23-28 (The Sabbath is made for man)*
Jesus respected the law, but was not limited by it. He had the inner freedom to act beyond the social, cultural and religious boundaries of his time. In doing so he was able to reach everyone—tax collectors, prostitutes, lepers and even gentiles.

■ *John 15:9-17 (God loves us deeply)*
Fear results from over-exaggerating what is expected of us. When we deepen our awareness of God's love for us, we begin to experience an inner confidence without which we can have no lasting security. Moreover, we can then learn to re-direct the energies we vainly spend in trying to counter our fears.

■ *Matthew 10:26-33 (The courage of our convictions)*
With God's protection and providence there is no need to be afraid. Understanding that enables us to be courageous in professing our faith and witnessing to the truth, no matter how intimidating the circumstances may be.

Further Comments

_____

_____

_____

_____

_____

_____

_____

_____

_____

_____

_____

_____

_____

_____

PRACTICAL SUGGESTION

◇◇◇ *As a rule we tend to keep our guard up and are afraid to let go. We don't trust our feelings and avoid spontaneity. It will help us in our prayer if we do what we can to trust our deepest selves and continually remind ourselves that God loves us. Talking with God as we would to a best friend will move us on from repeating set formulas written by others. If we focus on our breathing, we can make each breath a "thank-you" to the Spirit, the Breath of Life. Another suggestion is to place our hands palms upwards on our knees and, with our eyes fixed on them, allow them to reflect back to us our letting go of fear and our openness to whatever God surprises us with.*

SEVENS

DAILY PRAYER

Lord God, I thank you for giving me
a childlike enthusiasm and the ability
to enjoy the good things in life.
Show me how to embrace everything
with temperance and moderation.
Help me to see that running away
from pain does not lead to happiness.
Give me the wisdom to discover
that joy is to be found, not in the superficial,
but within the depths of my own heart. Amen.

Name It

My Name:	The Optimist
My Vice:	Gluttony
My God:	Ultimate Happiness
My Masks:	Planning, Togetherness, Generosity, Fantasy
My Need:	Balance
My Virtue:	Temperance

Claim It

Deep down I'm intemperate. That's my brokenness. I don't normally admit it, but I'm a glutton for more. What I want is a superabundance of the good things in life, of the things that are likely to bring me happiness. Nothing is ever enough. I consume things rather than savor and enjoy them. I take life in big gulps rather than in little sips. I emphasize the positive and minimize the negative. Basically, what I'm doing is trying to avoid pain and the emptiness inside.

Even though I move around a lot, essentially I live in my head. I'm very idealistic, concentrating on the good and rationalizing or trivializing the difficulties. I have lots of plans and schemes for doing good, but I gloss over the problems. I'm future-orientated, always anticipating life. The fact that I don't fully experience the pleasure of the present leads to my not being completely satisfied. I generally make sure I have so much to do that I'll never get bored. Indeed, my need for constant stimulation leads me, at times, to addictive behavior.

I look for distractions to keep me occupied and help me cope with painful realities. I find it hard to delay gratification. When I want things I want them now. My senses are so sharp that I can almost taste the enjoyment. The trouble is that I can also vividly imagine the intensity of pain, and I look for every possible diversion to avoid it. That's why I'm continually on the go and try not to get tied down to routine tasks. In effect, I'm running away from myself because I fear that, if I stop to look inside, I won't like what I see.

Lord God, slow me down long enough to discover the depth and beauty within. You have given me a childlike wonder at life, the blessing of good humor and a marvelous sense of fun. I am able to see the ridiculous side of life and make people laugh. That's a precious commodity in today's world. But I need help to realize that I do not have to search for happiness non-stop—that, if I cease my restless pursuit of it, happiness will surely find me. I need to discover that real joy is not dependent on outside circumstances but lies essentially within my own heart. Help me to dig beneath the surface so as to gain the true perspective of depth.

Tame It

We need to become more reflective and responsible, yet, paradoxically, our spiritual journey is from the inside out. Our natural curiosity and our attraction to constant change and the "quick-fix" make it very difficult for us to focus our attention when we come to pray. There are so many delightful possibilities and options to choose from that, given the opportunity, we attempt to pursue them all. However, we can slow down our mental games by "anchoring" ourselves in the real. We can do this, for example, by adopting a posture which ensures stillness and stops physical movement. Then we can begin.

The following suggestions for reflection and prayer, though not exhaustive, may help.

■ *Matthew 7:24-27 (Build on rock, not on sand)*
Staying on the surface of life is ultimately doomed to failure. Real growth and long-term happiness demand a rock-solid foundation of depth. Concentrating on the superficial is no way to build for the future.

■ *Mark 8:31-33 (Running away is not the answer)*
It is characteristic of us that when the going gets tough we tend to get going! Jesus refuses to throw in the towel when faced with difficulties and disappointments, and sends a clear message to those of us who do.

■ *Matthew 15:21-28 (Perseverance pays off)*
Our enthusiasm is generally short-lived. But when it comes to difficult life-issues and the healing of brokenness, it is essential to be persistent, to put up with the put-downs and stay with the pain. If we do, the chances are that, like the woman in the gospel, we will eventually go away happy.

■ *Mark 12:31 (Self-love is a condition for loving others)*
We are naturally gregarious. But we shouldn't forget that joy can be found in solitude as well. There is no need for us to fear being on our own. Solitude is not the same as loneliness and inner silence can enrich our understanding of ourselves.

■ *Matthew 14:22-33 (How to walk on water)*
We find it hard to believe someone will help us when we are in trouble. We have plan B always ready. But God continually surprises us. Even though we are afraid, God's caring presence encourages us to risk getting our feet wet.

Further Comments

_____

_____

_____

_____

_____

_____

_____

_____

_____

_____

_____

_____

_____

_____

_____

_____

_____

_____

_____

_____

_____

_____

PRACTICAL SUGGESTION

◇◇◇ *Since the present doesn't completely satisfy us, we are constantly planning for a more enjoyable future and trying to diffuse our pain by over-activity. But it pays off if we learn the art of staying in one place. One way is to sit comfortably with our hands resting gently on our knees, palms up. Instead of closing our eyes and letting the mind have free rein, it is useful to focus on our empty palms, a symbol of our openness to the spirit and of our willingness to let go of our consumer mentality and our materialistic approach to life. Or we could savor the scent of a flower, slowly caress the surface of a leaf, or sit by a lake and feel ourselves part of something greater than ourselves.*

EIGHTS

DAILY PRAYER

Lord God, I thank you for giving me
a tremendous passion for life,
a powerful sense of justice
and the energy to get things done.
Help me always to protect the weak
and champion the oppressed.
Give me a heart filled with compassion
so that I may experience the strength
that comes through gentleness
and the respect that comes through love. Amen.

Name It

My Name:	The Leader
My Vice:	Lust
My God:	The Omnipotent Judge
My Masks:	Revenge, Control, Friendship, Possession
My Need:	Tenderness
My Virtue:	Innocence/Childlikeness

Claim It

Deep down I'm lustful. That's my brokenness. Pleasure for me is bound up with control. I exploit people because of my passion to dominate and possess. I violate their space, use them without shame and humiliate them without guilt. At my worst I simply don't consider how vulnerable people can be and have no respect for their feelings. I satisfy my instincts and enjoy life's pleasures without too many hang-ups. I can be cruel rather than kind. Sometimes I punish people disproportionately for the mistakes that they've made. When I put forward high standards of morality I expect others to live up to them without really feeling obliged to do so myself.

I like to keep tabs on things, to check up on even the most trivial details. It's my way of not letting things get out of hand. I value my independence and prefer to be dominant in my relationships. I'm very possessive and find it hard to compromise or adapt. I tend to bully people and don't respect those who will not fight back. I see things in black and white. People are either for me or against me, friends or enemies.

Without realizing it, I find myself pushing people around. I'm generally insensitive to the hurt I'm causing. I substitute aggressive behavior for playfulness and sexual activity for intimacy. I have no problem about fighting "dirty." I'm direct, often to the point of rudeness, and use strong language to emphasize what I'm trying to say. I don't pull any punches. I say what I mean and mean what I say. I tend to confront rather than communicate. I readily spit out my anger in the belief that attack is the best form of defense.

Lord God, I know you have given me an enormous passion for life, for love and for justice. It comes out in the way I generally take the side of the underdog. But I have to avoid becoming a self-appointed judge and jury, always willing to retaliate when I think the balance needs to be redressed. I have to accept my vulnerability and let others see the tender and more gentle side of me which I keep so well hidden beneath my deliberately tough exterior.

Tame It

Our inner journey demands an openness to God and to other people. We need to strive to integrate action and contemplation, and to balance passionate expression and a refusal to self-disclose. Since we generally live in the present we find it easy to be immediately present to God in prayer. For us this involves a centering of our selves, an emptying of thoughts and feelings, a letting go of activity and a stillness of loving presence which transcends our everyday wants and needs.

As gut people we naturally want to be doing and are suspicious of inactivity. But our best prayer is that of simple presence. Paradoxically it brings us both a heightened sensitivity and a calming inner tranquility.

The following suggestions for reflection and prayer, though not exhaustive, may help.

■ *Luke 4:16-23 (Setting the downtrodden free)*
We have been given power so that we can help those who are powerless. Our strength should be used to help the weak and the marginalized. Our words can speak for those who have no voice and our deeds support those who need protection.

■ *Matthew 14:13-21 (Feeding the hungry)*
The most characteristic gut reaction of Jesus is one of compassion. Whenever people are troubled, harassed, rejected or in difficulty, Jesus doesn't have to think about what to do. Without hesitation he reacts with tenderness and mercy.

■ *John 13:1-17 (The washing of the feet)*
Jesus sees the ministry of compassion as essentially one of service. Peter, who believes in hierarchy and in power, refuses to allow Jesus to wash his feet. But he is told bluntly that unless he is willing to let himself be ministered to, he cannot hope to be of service to others.

■ *Luke 4:1-13 (The temptations in the wilderness)*
We are all tempted to misuse power for our own ends rather than use it for the benefit of others. Jesus refused to abuse his power in any self-serving way. Strength is given to us not for show but for service.

■ *Matthew 18:21-35 (The unforgiving debtor)*
Our natural "eye-for-an-eye" attitude involves payback for injury and punishment for offense. This parable, however, highlights the importance of forgiveness. We cannot continue to nurse our grievances. We need to let them go.

Further Comments

_____

_____

_____

_____

_____

_____
_____
_____
_____
_____
_____
_____
_____
_____
_____
_____
_____
_____
_____
_____
_____
_____

PRACTICAL SUGGESTION

◇◇◇ *Since we have so much energy at our disposal it can help if we harness this in our prayer. Praying with our body allows us to experience the strength of action and the gentleness of contemplation. Through our body we can move beyond our daily concerns to the deeper realms of the spirit. In particular, we can use the tactile to help us experience the divine. Sculpture or pottery, for example, can slow us down and help us get in touch with our deepest energies and feelings. It could also help to surrender ourselves creatively in painting, using color, line, texture and shape to bridge the gap between our outer and inner worlds.*

NINES

DAILY PRAYER

Lord God, I thank you for giving me
the gift of gentleness and
a profound tranquility of heart.
Help me to own my deepest feelings
without losing my inner peace,
and to appreciate my own importance
without ever selling myself short.
Above all, show me how to cope
with life's conflicts and problems
with a confident trust in your love. Amen.

Name It

My Name:	The Mediator
My Vice:	Sloth
My God:	Ultimate Peace
My Masks:	Indolence, Addiction, Partnership, Union
My Need:	Action
My Virtue:	Diligence

Claim It

Deep down I'm slothful. That's my brokenness. I don't even bother to try to cover it up. There's no need to, since I have effectively persuaded myself and everybody else that I'm just easy-going. But the truth is that I try to avoid all conflict and am prepared to settle for peace at any price. I don't like to be upset and am always willing to paper over the cracks. To avoid facing problems I tend to sweep them under the carpet, denying that they exist, and make molehills out of mountains to soften the pain. I regularly settle for less.

Basically, I'm cynical about human nature. I see nobody as a big deal, not even myself. I have a poor self-image and am not convinced of my own importance.

The core of my laziness probably lies in my belief that nothing really matters and that, consequently, there's no great harm in taking the path of least resistance. I much prefer to get on with the bits and pieces rather than the things which demand responsibility and commitment. It is hard for me to make decisions and I tend to procrastinate. I regularly put off difficult tasks and become vague or obstinate when people try to pin me down. My lack of response is a form of passive aggression which I find very effective. Because I'm not a self-starter I'm inclined to be addictive. I generally have to look for stimulation outside of myself.

Lord God, I've spent my life trying to deny my feelings. I've attempted to shut them down to avoid the pain they bring. This is how I try to control my environment and gain some power over the ebb and flow of my life. I am "prone" to inertia, if you'll forgive the pun! I'm afraid of being overwhelmed by uncontrollable emotions. In particular, I swallow my anger and let it fester within. Help me to accept my emotions and allow my gut feelings to surface and give me life.

Tame It

We try so hard to manage our emotions at every moment that we can miss the beauty, the intensity and the thrill of the present. When we over-value being calm and peaceful the danger is that we find it difficult to become excited or enthusiastic about anything. We have to stop putting ourselves down and continually defining ourselves in terms of what we think others expect of us. Deepening our awareness that we are loved by God precisely for who we are can help us become more self-confident and independent. We will not then feel so overwhelmed by life's difficulties and, instead of withdrawing from the scene, will become actively involved, determine our priorities and accept responsibility for the decisions we make.

The following suggestions for reflection and prayer, though not exhaustive, may help.

■ *John 18:32-33 (We are not alone)*
Our lack of a real sense of our selves brings with it a deep loneliness. We feel empty inside, as if there is nobody at home. But
Jesus reminds us that God's Spirit dwells within each of us.
Once we realize that we, too, are important and that we are
never alone, we will not be afraid to make the inner journey to
encounter the God in our hearts.

■ *John 5:1-16 (Sitting by the pool)*
The sick man at the House of Mercy (Bethesda) spent 38 years
at the Sheep Pool waiting for a helping hand. When Jesus saw
him there he told hm to get up and walk. If we are prepared to
seize the opportunities which come our way, we can find healing. On the other hand, if we just sit and wait for something to
happen, life may simply pass us by.

■ *Luke 8:22-25 (Calming the storm)*
Life is not all plain sailing. It has its inevitable ups and downs.
But if we trust in God's providence we will be at peace even in
the midst of conflict and turmoil.

■ *John 21:1-8 (Throw out the nets)*
Our trust in God's providence can help point us in the right direction. Even when we think our contribution is not worth the
effort, God encourages us to make a start. When we are prepared to work with others and do our bit, the results can often
surprise us.

■ *Matthew 10:28-31 (The hairs on our head are counted)*
Nobody is insignificant in God's sight. We are loved and cared
for individually. Recognizing our value and worth is essential
to being able to act autonomously. Understanding our dignity
leads to greater personal freedom.

Further Comments

_____

_____

_____

_____

PRACTICAL SUGGESTION

◇◇◇ *Since we live in the immediate world of the here-and-now, with all its conflict and all its calm, it can help us greatly to get in touch with the still center within, where all is gift and harmony. To achieve this we could sit quietly in a church, a prayer room or some other peaceful spot. We don't need to use words, though the "Jesus Prayer" or a mantra may help give us focus. It is enough to enjoy being in God's presence. We mustn't mistake this for daydreaming or idleness. It is a letting go. The result is often a combination of being sensitively alert while being peacefully serene. When we risk losing ourselves in God, we find God in our deepest selves.*

6

LOVE IN BROKENNESS

We have written this book as a guide—a pointer to the way the Enneagram can help us unearth some of the treasures buried within each of our hearts. We have deliberately kept it brief and tried to be as clear as possible so as to avoid confusing our readers with a mass of detail. If you have found it helpful, we suggest you read some of the other books available on the subject. Better still, we recommend you go to a workshop where you can experience for yourself the reality of what we have been saying about the nine different types.

In any event, we hope that with the aid of the Enneagram you will be in a better position to discover your true self. It will help if we don't expect too much. It is not a shovel, to be used to dig deep and make a big hole in our soul. That hole is probably big enough already. Rather it is a sophisticated and nuanced instrument which will allow us to see the reality of who we are without destroying it in the process. Moreover, while the Enneagram is undoubtedly a valuable way of looking at ourselves and others, it is not so necessary that we cannot do without it. It is, after all, just one tool among many.

Our hope is that as a result of using the Enneagram each of us will become more compassionate, more understanding of our own and other people's inner pain, more discerning about the real face concealed behind the perennial smile, more tolerant of our own faults and failings as well as those of others, more patient with the slow progress all of us make in dealing with our compulsive energies and, above all, as we Irish say, more *flaithiúlach* ("lavish beyond measure") in our love for ourselves and for every other human being with whom we come in contact.

Love, after all, is the very reason for our existence. We were loved into existence and it is love that keeps us there. Essentially, we will never cease to be because God's love will always enfold us, in joy and in pain, in good times and in bad, in life and beyond death. That's the wonderful thing about our knowledge of God gained from Jesus. God loves us even in our sinfulness. "What proves God loves us is that while we were still sinners Christ died for us." (Romans 5:8) No matter what our brokenness, no matter what blind alleys we choose, God still loves us.

When we were little children, many of us were told, "Remember, God sees you." This was usually said to keep us from getting into mischief and was generally interpreted by us as an invasion of our privacy. But, as some of us later found out, what it really meant was that God was head over heels in love with us and simply couldn't stop looking at us! In a very real sense, we are so utterly loved that we can never step out of that loving embrace. Nothing we can do can stop God from loving us. Even in our brokenness we are still loved. As the beautiful Spanish proverb puts it, "God can write straight with crooked lines." God is infinitely patient with both our weakness and our willfulness.

That kind of love is both a consolation and a challenge. It allows us to experience a deep inner peace. It unifies the divisions within our hearts. But it also calls us forth, encouraging us to grow and develop. The love which brought us into existence can also bring us home—to personal maturity, wholeness and holiness.

There will come a time when we will know ourselves even as we are known by God (cf. 1 Corinthians 13:12). Too often in the midst of our daily cares and concerns we see our brokenness more clearly than we see our giftedness. But God has a different perspective. God looks into our innermost being and rejoices to see the divine image reflected back. In God's eyes we are not broken but fundamentally whole.

Holding Tight and Letting Go

It is in losing ourselves that we really find ourselves (cf. Matthew 10:39). It is in letting go that we receive a full measure. But before we can let go, we must first have something to let go of. This means that we need to know what our fixation, compulsion or addiction really is, have accepted it in as complete a fashion as we can, and *then*, in freedom, let it go. This is not an overnight thing; it will take time. Indeed, in a real sense it takes a lifetime. Our lives are a continual series of little deaths, a daily letting go, a surrendering to the Mysterious Other who gifts us with life each waking moment. For us, that other is God.

A couple of personal stories may help. A good many years ago Eddie took on too many responsibilities and suffered the inevitable consequence.

About fifteen years ago I overworked myself to the point of exhaustion. In my efforts to stay in control, I had worked so hard that I lost what I wanted most. My system just broke down. I was like a scalded cat, all motor movement but with no central coordination. I couldn't speak and I lost the use of my hands and feet. The doctor recommended a complete rest so I had to go to bed. My mind was clear; I knew exactly what was going on. The trouble was I could do absolutely nothing about it. In spite of all the care and attention I received from the members of my community, nothing seemed to work. About a week later one of our older priests, James (who is now dead), returned from a visit home. He must have thought the house was quieter than usual because he asked where I was and immediately paid me a visit. When he saw me, James gave a wry little smile. Then, without a word, he just sat on the side of my bed, gathered me into his arms and hugged me tight. Something snapped inside and I let go. It seemed to be the easiest thing to do. The floodgates opened and I was back to normal. Only when I was prepared to let go and be held was I capable of being healed.

Éilís works with children who have been broken and hurt in all kinds of ways and has been able to help them out of her own experience of brokenness and of being loved.

In our work we find that no two days are ever the same. As John Denver might put it, some days are diamonds and some days are stones. This particular day had been a gigantic boulder—an obstacle course in love. In the evening I decided to go to the parish church for Mass and took one of the children with me. As I sat there, halfway down the church, joining with the priest and people in thanksgiving to God, I cradled my little six-year-old in my lap. My arms embraced her, unconsciously trying to protect her from any further pain, any further hurt. I remembered how just that morning she had taken her doll and systematically ripped it apart, dropping the bits and pieces all over the house—in the bedroom, on the stairs and all along the hall. She'd hardly spoken since she arrived and this was probably the only way she had of telling us how broken she was. I couldn't keep my heart from crying as I held her close. I looked down at her cradled there and said: "You poor little mite—you're so broken. But don't worry, you're safe now. With God's help, together we'll pick up the pieces."

Our wounds have to be touched if they are ever going to be healed. For that to happen we need to let ourselves be gathered up in love. The image Jesus gives is of God wanting to gather us up like a mother hen would gather her chicks (cf. Luke 13:34). This involves a double movement of love on our part. In surrendering ourselves to God's love we *let go* of our compulsive and fixed view of the world, and *hold on tight* to love. The gospel message is that we are saved more by the love we share than by the love we show. God first loved us, and loves us unconditionally. When we hold on to that love and rest in it, we are truly blessed and grow in holiness. Then, in our giftedness, we can open our hearts and share that love with each other.

BIBLIOGRAPHY

The books listed here are all very helpful. There are, of course, many other books on psychology, spirituality and related subjects that are particularly useful, but we have concentrated on those that are specifically about the Enneagram and are quite readily available.

Beesing, Maria; Nogosek, Robert J.; and O'Leary, Patrick. *The Enneagram: A Journey of Self-Discovery.* Denville, N.J.: Dimension Books, 1984.

Callahan, William J. *The Enneagram for Youth.* Chicago: Loyola University Press, 1992.

Hannan, Peter. *Nine Faces of God.* Dublin: Columba Press, 1992.
Hurley, Kathleen V.; and Dobson, Theodore E. *What's My Type?: Use the Enneagram System of Nine Personality Types to Discover Your Best Self.* New York: HarperCollins, 1991.

Kelly, Mary Helen. *Skin Deep: Designer Clothes by God.* Memphis: Monastery of St. Clare, 1990.
Keyes, Margaret Frings, *Emotions and the Enneagram: Working Through Your Shadow Life Script.* Muir Beach, Calif.: Molysdatur Publications, 1990.
Keyes, Margaret Frings. *The Enneagram Relationship Workbook: A Self and Partnership Assessment Guide.* Muir Beach, Calif.: Molysdatur Publications, 1991.

Metz, Barbara; and Burchill, John. *The Enneagram and Prayer: Discovering Our True Selves Before God.* Denville, N.J.: Dimension Books, 1987.

Naranjo, Claudio. *Ennea-Type Structures: Self-Analysis for the Seeker.* Nevada City: Gateways/IDHHB, 1990.

Nogosek, Robert. *Nine Portraits of Jesus: Discovering Jesus Through the Enneagram.* Denville, N.J.: Dimension Books, 1987.

Palmer, Helen. *The Enneagram: Understanding Yourself and the People Around You.* New York: Harper & Row, 1988.

Riso, Don Richard. *Personality Types: Using the Enneagram for Self-Discovery.* Boston: Houghton Mifflin, 1987.

Riso, Don Richard. *The Practical Guide to Personality Types: Understanding the Enneagram.* Northamptonshire: Aquarian Press, 1990.

Rohr, Richard; and Ebert, Andreas. Translated by Peter Heinegg. *Discovering the Enneagram: An Ancient Tool for a New Spiritual Journey.* New York: Crossroad, 1990.

Rohr, Richard; Ebert, Andreas, and others. Translated by Peter Heinegg. *Experiencing the Enneagram.* New York: Crossroad, 1992.

Thomson, Clarence. *The Enneagram Educator* (quarterly newsletter). 115 East Armour Blvd. Kansas City, Mo. 64111

Tickerhoof, B. *Conversion & the Enneagram: Transformation of the Self in Christ.* Denville, N.J.: Dimension Books, 1991.

Zuercher, Suzanne. *Enneagram Spirituality.* Notre Dame, Ind.: Ave Maria Press, 1992.